A GCSE Resource

Edited by

Roy Blatchford and Jackie Head

UNWIN

HYMAN

Published in 1990 by
UNWIN HYMAN LIMITED
15/17 Broadwick Street
London W1V 1FP

British Library Cataloguing in Publication Data

Writing and response.
1. Secondary schools. Curriculum subjects: English language. Writing skills. Teaching
I. Blatchford, Roy II. Head, Jackie
808'.042'071

ISBN 0-04-448093-8

Designed by Bob Wright
Typeset by MS Filmsetting Limited, Frome, Somerset
Printed and bound in Great Britain by
Butler & Tanner Ltd, Frome and London

Contents

Acknowledgements

The editors and publisher are grateful to the following for permission to reproduce the material in this book.

'A Policeman's Lot' © Wendy Cope, first published in *Making Cocoa For Kingsley Amis* reproduced by permission of Faber & Faber, 1986.

A Poet's Lot © Wendy Cope, 1988.

'The Interview' © Adèle Geras, 1989.

Playing the Window Game © Adèle Geras, 1989.

'Profile: Kenneth Branagh' © Fionnuala McHugh, first published in Options Magazine, November 1987.

Lines of Communication © Fionnuala McHugh, 1989.

'White Peak Farm: Gran' © Berlie Doherty, reproduced by permission of the BBC.

Gran: an Adaptation for Television © Berlie Doherty, 1989.

'A Head for Figures' © Joan Lingard, taken from *Rags and Riches*, reproduced by permission of Penguin Books Ltd, 1988.

Other Worlds © Joan Lingard, 1989.

'Free Dinners' © Farrukh Dhondy, taken from *Come To Mecca*, 1978, reproduced by permission of William Collins Sons & Co.

A Writer Talking © Farrukh Dhondy, 1989.

Wendy Cope

A POET'S LOT

Wendy Cope

Wendy Cope was born in 1945 in Erith, Kent and educated at Farringtons School in Chislehurst and St. Hilda's College, Oxford. She worked as a primary school teacher for many years and is now a full-time freelance writer, living in London. In 1987 she won a Cholmondeley Award for poetry.

My first poem was composed when I was six years old. It was about my teddy bear, Roger, and I wrote it at school because we were told to write a poem. After that we weren't told to write any more poems, so I didn't, for quite a while. At this age poetry wasn't important to me but I already loved books. As soon as I was able to read to myself, reading became my favourite occupation. Before long I began writing stories of my own in a special exercise book. I told people that I was going to be a writer when I grew up.

The poetry we did at primary school mostly seemed to be about nature and fairies. It didn't interest me much. In my elocution lessons I had to memorise Christina Rossetti's 'Who Has Seen the Wind?' and then I had to practise reciting it, with lots and lots of expression. To this day I can't stand that poem, nor can I bear to hear anyone reciting anything with lots of expression. It was a nice surprise, a few years ago, to discover that, as well as perpetrating 'Who Has Seen the Wind?', Christina Rossetti wrote wonderful, heart-rending poems about love and death—subjects we didn't do at primary school.

At home I was exposed to a different kind of poetry. My father, born in 1885 and nearly 60 years old when I came along, loved to recite the poems he had learned when he was young. My sister and I, to tell the truth, weren't all that keen on being quiet and listening to 'The Charge of the Light Brigade' or 'The Burial of Sir John Moore after Corunna' yet again. But once he got going you couldn't stop him, and over the years I grew fond of the poems. Edward Fitzgerald's translation of 'The Rubaiyat of Omar Khayyam', a favourite of my father's, remains a special favourite of mine too.

When I was 14 I wrote a few more poems. They are dreadful. One is about Princess Margaret's wedding and the others express my unquenchable love for a pop singer. This phase didn't last long. By now I had stopped writing stories (except when told to at school) and forgotten about wanting to be a writer. So many people wanted to be writers—who was I to think I could make it? But I was beginning to realise that I really did like poetry—some of it, anyway—bits of Hardy and Yeats on our 'O' level syllabus and then, in the sixth form, Keats. I fell in love with Keats and decided I would like to marry a poet and be his soulmate.

After school, I went to university and read history. Very occasionally I would pick up a poetry book for half an hour. I wrote nothing except compulsory history essays. By the time I left, I hated history and had absolutely no idea what I wanted to do with my life. For want of anything better, I took a job as a primary school teacher.

Five years later, at the age of 27, I began writing poems again and have continued to do so ever since. Looking back, it seems to me that there are three reasons why this happened at that particular moment. My interest in poetry had been re-kindled by the work I was doing with the children at school. I was living alone for the first time. And I had recently entered psychoanalysis because I was very depressed after the death of my father. Psychoanalysis was giving me a new awareness of my real feelings. There were things I wanted to explore and express and there were no longer any flatmates around to talk to. One Saturday afternoon I sat down and wrote a poem, two more the next day, and so it went on.

These early poems were in free verse, short, lyrical and intense. They used images from the natural world to express what seemed to be happening to me. Several of them are about winter trees waiting for the spring. The impulse to read poetry also came back to me. T. S. Eliot, Sylvia Plath, Ted Hughes and Philip Larkin are among the poets whose work was important to me at this time. I bought *The New Oxford Book of English Verse* and dipped at random into the poetry of other centuries. It was all very exciting.

But poets need the company of other poets. Who could I talk to about this new interest? A few of my friends had read English at university—they would know all about poetry, wouldn't they? Sad to say, most of them changed the subject as quickly as possible. Luckily, I did find one person I could talk to—a colleague at work, who had published poems when he was younger. Then I heard about the Arvon Foundation, which runs open courses in Devon and Yorkshire for people who want to write. Over the next five years, Arvon courses, and an evening class at Goldsmith's College in London, brought me into contact with people who shared my interest in poetry. Some of them had an important influence on the development of my work.

Showing poems to other people is difficult at first but it gets easier. Nowadays I have several poet friends who look at new work for me. Though their comments are often valuable, I always bear in mind that no-one is infallible. If one of them says something that echoes my own doubts about a line, or a whole poem, I accept that further work is needed. But if I'm sure about something, I stick to it, no matter what my advisers say. The last line of my poem 'Tich Miller' was disliked by the first six people who read it. I thought hard and decided not to change it and I'm sure, now, that the decision was right.

By the time I found my way to these courses and classes, I had begun sending work to little poetry magazines, in the hope of getting published. When someone first told me that my work was promising and that I should try and get it into print, I was pleased, in a way, but also a bit sad. Next day I went out, bought some paints, and began experimenting with them, safe in the knowledge that no-one would ever tell me I had any talent for painting. Until then writing poetry had been something I did purely for its own sake, because I felt like it and found it satisfying. To begin with I had no intention of showing the poems to anyone, let alone trying to publish them. The idea of appearing in print is, of course, appealing but I was afraid this new ambition would spoil everything. I wouldn't be writing for myself any longer but to impress editors and the rest of the world. This was the beginning of a struggle that has been going on ever since. The desire for recognition is inevitably a threat to the integrity of one's writing and it is impossible for me to write anything that's any good unless I manage to put it aside.

What happens, fortunately, is that I sometimes get into a mood where I just don't care. I have an idea for a poem and I really want to write it, regardless of whether anyone anywhere is going to approve of it or want to publish it. Very often, when I am composing a poem, I feel that this is one I can show to very few people—perhaps to nobody at all—because it is too scurrilous or obscene or offensive or soppy. Even so, I don't want to stop working until it's finished. Weeks, months or years later, I may decide to publish it after all.

The early drafts of my poems are usually written in large black hardback notebooks. The advantage of using a book is that individual pages can't get lost. If a poem goes through many drafts—and some of mine go through fifty or more—it's important to be able to look back and see if it is improving or getting worse. In this respect writers are more fortunate than painters or sculptors. If we ruin something we're working on, we are free simply to put a line through it and return to an earlier version, which hasn't been covered over or chipped away.

When I think a poem is more or less right, I type it out. With a tremendous feeling of satisfaction, I sit back and read it through. Then, most often, I notice that there is at least one line that really won't do. I begin crossing out and scribbling on the typescript. I type the amended version. Then I make more alterations. And so it goes on.

Now and again a poem arrives quickly, needing little work. Sometimes, nowadays, I make them up in my head and don't write them down until they're finished. This is a helpful development because it means I can work while I'm walking round the park, or swimming, or standing at a bus stop. But even in my head the poems usually go through a number of drafts.

People sometimes ask me how I choose the form for a poem. Some of mine are in free verse, many of them make use of traditional forms—the sonnet, the villanelle, the triolet, and so on. The answer is that a poem has to find its form by a process of trial and error. Some of my villanelles began life as triolets, the rondeau redoublés were both, at one stage, villanelles, and several of my rhyming poems were initially in free verse.

'A Policeman's Lot' is one of these. I first had the idea for this peom when I came across the sentence that is printed at the top, the epigraph. It comes in Ted Hughes's introduction to *What Rhymes With Secret?*, one of Sandy Brownjohn's books for teachers. Though it struck me as a true and helpful statement, it also conjured up a mental picture of a lot of little men in blue uniforms running around inside the poet, trying to prevent him from composing poems. In the case of Ted Hughes, I reflected, this would probably be a difficult job. I imagined a disgruntled member of the anti-poetry squad complaining about his work and began playing with this idea in prose and in free verse. Luckily, I happened to have tickets for a performance of Gilbert and Sullivan's *The Pirates of Penzance* the following evening. As soon as the Sergeant began to sing his song—with the refrain 'A policeman's lot is not a happy one'—I knew what to do with my idea of the previous evening. After that, the actual writing of the poem was quite easy, though this doesn't mean—as you will see from the draft included here on pages 12 and 13—that there wasn't any crossing out and revision.

However, I am afraid you will not learn very much from this draft, except that poets do not always have good handwriting. Mine isn't always as bad as this scribble. I seem to have developed a special illegible scrawl for use in my notebook, perhaps because I don't want anybody to be able to read things until I feel confident about them. But it has its drawbacks. Sometimes I have lost a whole line or stanza because I couldn't make head or tail of it myself.

People sometimes refer to 'A Policeman's Lot' as a parody but they are wrong to do so. I call it a literary joke. It is a mistake to assume that all literary jokes can accurately be called parodies. Some of my poems *are* parodies. The two entitled 'Nursery Rhyme', for example, are parodies of Wordsworth and T. S. Eliot. 'Budgie Finds His Voice' is a parody of Ted Hughes. In these poems I have attempted to imitate the way another poet writes—with careful attention to his use of rhythm, choice of vocabulary and so on—in such a way that my poem conveys what it is about this writer's work that sometimes makes me smile. A successful parody should make the reader laugh and think, 'Yes it is sometimes a bit like that.' But when I poke fun at other writers, it is mostly affectionate fun. If I didn't enjoy their work, I wouldn't know enough about it to be able to send them up.

Not long after 'A Policeman's Lot' was finished, I sent it to the editor of *Poetry Review* and he accepted it for publication. My poems don't always get accepted by the first editor I send them to but these days most of the things I want to see in print are taken by somebody, sooner or later.

It was not always so. My first attempts to get published, mentioned earlier, met with no success at all and this continued to be the case for six years. Poets often have difficulty making the initial breakthrough into print. In my case the difficulty was compounded by the fact that most of the poems I was sending off were not (I can see with hindsight) all that wonderful. Periodically I would decide to give up all this poetry nonsense. What was the point? Even if you succeeded, you wouldn't make any money. But it turned out that I had reached a point where giving up would not be easy. Whatever I decided, poems came along. If I tried to ignore them, they kept me awake at night.

So I kept on working at them. I got better at it. Eventually *The Times Literary Supplement* took a poem, then another. At around the same time Priapus Press brought out my first booklet, *Across the City*. Over the next two or three years it gradually became clear that I would be able to publish a full-length book but I wasn't in any hurry. The longer I waited, it seemed to me, the better the book would be.

When *Making Cocoa for Kingsley Amis* finally appeared in 1986, it received a great deal of publicity and most of the reviews were good. In this respect I was very fortunate—many poetry books are published invisibly and sell badly. Mine reached the bestseller lists and brought in its wake many offers of work of various kinds. By now a part-time teacher, I was able, at last, to give up teaching altogether.

However, 1986 was, in some ways, a difficult year. It seemed that people were ringing up all the time, asking me to do things I'd never done before—things I didn't feel at all confident about. At times I thought the pressure would drive me mad. There were so many decisions to make. Did I want to be on television? (Mostly I said no to this.) Could I write the article they wanted? Had I got time to judge this or that poetry competition? All thought of writing any poems went right out of the window.

Now that things have quietened down a bit, I'm happier. Most of my time is spent on journalism, giving readings, perusing competition entries, or taking part in radio programmes—I need to do these things to earn a living. But every so often—though I am always afraid it will stop happening—a line comes into my head and I find myself working on a poem.

PUBLICATIONS

Across the City, Priapus Press, 1980
Poetry Introduction 5, Faber & Faber, 1982
Making Cocoa For Kingsley Amis, Faber & Faber, 1986
Twiddling Your Thumbs: Hand rhymes for children, Faber & Faber, 1986

Is That The New Moon?: Poems by women. (Editor) Collins, *Teen Track* series, 1989

A POLICEMAN'S LOT

Wendy Cope

The progress of any writer is marked by those moments when he manages to outwit his own inner police system. Ted Hughes

Oh, once I was a policeman young and merry (young and merry),
Controlling crowds and fighting petty crime (petty crime)
But now I work on matters literary (litererry)
And I am growing old before my time ('fore my time).
No, the imagination of a writer (of a writer)
Is not the sort of beat a chap would choose (chap would choose)
And they've assigned me a prolific blighter ('lific blighter) –
I'm patrolling the unconscious of Ted Hughes.

It's not the sort of beat a chap would choose (chap would choose) –
Patrolling the unconscious of Ted Hughes.

All our leave was cancelled in the lambing season (lambing season)
When bitter winter froze the drinking trough (drinking trough)
For our commander stated, with good reason (with good reason),
That that's the kind of thing that starts him off (starts him off).
But anything with four legs causes trouble (causes trouble) –
It's worse than organising several zoos (several zoos),
Not to mention mythic creatures in the rubble (in the rubble),
Patrolling the unconscious of Ted Hughes.

It's worse than organising several zoos (several zoos),
Patrolling the unconscious of Ted Hughes.

Although it's disagreeable and stressful (bull and stressful)
Attempting to avert poetic thought ('etic thought),
I could boast of times when I have been successful (been successful)
And conspiring compound epithets were caught ('thets were caught).
But the poetry statistics in this sector (in this sector)
Are enough to make a copper turn to booze (turn to booze)
And I do not think I'll make it to inspector (to inspector),
Patrolling the unconscious of Ted Hughes.

It's enough to make a copper turn to booze (turn to booze) –
Patrolling the unconscious of Ted Hughes.

(after W. S. Gilbert)

Response

A POET'S LOT

- 'The poetry we did at primary school mostly seemed to be about nature and fairies.' What have been your own experiences of poetry both at Primary and Secondary school?

- Wendy Cope writes about her father's love of reciting poems he had learned when he was young. What poems or lines of poetry can you recite off by heart? What are your views on learning poems by heart? Does it help you appreciate a poem?

- What reasons does Wendy Cope give for her starting to write poetry as an adult?

- Look up in *The New Oxford Book of English Verse* poems by T. S. Eliot, Sylvia Plath, Ted Hughes and Philip Larkin. Talk about their work with another student.

- What are the poet's views on the subject of showing her poems to other people?

- In what way, according to Wendy Cope, is the writer more fortunate than the painter or sculptor? Do you agree with her?

- Wendy Cope mentions different forms ot poems: sonnet, villanelle, triolet, rondeau, free verse. Research what each of these looks like on the page, and find an example of each.

- 'Some of my poems are parodies'. What does the word 'parody' mean? Can you think of examples in literature (or in film/on television) that you have come across? Discuss these in groups.

A POLICEMAN'S LOT

- Wendy Cope suggests that the inspiration for her poem came from two sources:
  (i) 'The progress of any writer is marked by those moments when he manages to outwit his own inner police system.' (Ted Hughes)
  (ii) When a felon's not engaged in his employment (his employment)
  Or maturing his felonious little plans (little plans),
  His capacity for innocent enjoyment ('cent enjoyment)
  Is just as great as any honest man's (honest man's).
  Our feeling when we difficulty smother ('culty smother)
  When constabulary duty's to be done (to be done),
  Ah, take one consideration with another (with another)
  A policeman's lot is not a happy one (happy one).

  Explain what you think Ted Hughes means. What similarities do you notice between the song above and Wendy Cope's poem? Do you find her version effective?

- The poet Ted Hughes has also written:
  'So it is with most words. They belong to several of the senses at once, as if each one had eyes, ears and tongue, or ears and fingers and a body to move with. It is this little goblin in a word which is its life and its poetry, and it is this goblin which the poet has to have under control'.
  Write a short review of 'A Policeman's Lot', with references to the above quotation.

- What do you think this poem manages to convey about its subject? What is the 'tone' of the poem, and does the style match the content?

- Look carefully at the poet's draft manuscript (page 12). (As Wendy Cope says, the handwriting sometimes defeats *her*!) What differences are there between the draft and the final version? Why might the poet have made the changes which she did?

- Which 'poetic devices'—for example, metaphor, repetition, rhyme—can you identify in the poem? Why are they used and to what effect?

- Write your own poem in the same style as 'A Policeman's Lot'. Think about the following as you are drafting and re-drafting:
  — Does the subject matter fit the form chosen?
  — Does it scan correctly?
  — Is the vocabulary exactly right, or are there some words which don't quite fit?
  — Are the lines and verses in the best order?
  — Does the poem say all you want to say about the topic chosen?

  Having asked and answered these questions yourself, share your poem with another student. What are their comments? Re-draft any parts which you think you could now improve.

Oh once I was a ~~[illegible]~~ policeman young and merry
(young and merry)

Controlling crowds and fighting petty crime
(petty crime)

But now I work at nothing [illegible]
(thing)

And I am going old before my time
('fore my time).

~~Probably the success~~ No, the important [illegible] of a [illegible]
(of a [illegible])

Is that the act of ~~[illegible]~~ being [illegible] ~~[illegible]~~ [illegible] clever
(I [illegible] clever)

And my crossword — a [illegible] blog [illegible]
(I [illegible] blog [illegible])

I'm perfectly the [illegible] of Ted Hughes
(of Ted Hughes)

Chs. Its not the [illegible] of ~~[illegible]~~ being [illegible] clever
(I [illegible])

Probably the [illegible] of Ted Hughes.

Cerebration

Its worse than ongoing since 2005
(since 2000)
Patrolling the environs of Ted Hughes:

Our licence was cancelled [illegible]

[illegible]

And our [illegible] in good [illegible]
([illegible])

[illegible]

It's worse than ongoing since 2005

[illegible]

Patrolling the environs of Ted
Hughes
(of Ted Hughes)

Adèle Geras

PLAYING THE WINDOW GAME

I was born in Jerusalem in 1944 and spent my early childhood in many countries, including North Borneo and the Gambia. I studied French and Spanish at St. Hilda's College, Oxford, (at exactly the same time that Wendy Cope was there studying.) I've been an actress/singer and a teacher of French, but I now write full-time. I live in Manchester with my husband and two daughters, aged 17 and 11. I'm a fanatical knitter and love going to the movies.

Whenever anyone asks me what my favourite book is, I always say either Jane Eyre *or* Little Women. *Here is a list, though, of writers whose work I always a) find admirable and b) enjoy hugely. They are in no order of merit, but simply written as they occur to me:*

Marcel Proust, Emil Zola, Anton Chekhov, F. Scott Fitzgerald, Isaac Bashevis Singer, A. S. Byatt, Maurice Sendak, Penelope Lively, Fay Weldon, Russell Hoban, Charlotte Bronte, Jan Mark, Jane Gardam, Jean Ure, Stephen King, P. D. James, Ruth Rendall, Raymond Chandler, Evelyn Waugh, Franz Kafka, Robert Westall, Judy Blume, Betsy Byars . . .

Before the beginning

Wherever I go, I glance into windows. I've done it for as long as I can remember. Whether I'm walking or on a bus or train, my head is permanently turned to one side, looking for the possibility of a glimpse, however brief, of other lives. Some people never draw their curtains, others pull them tightly around themselves as soon as dusk falls, but even then you sometimes catch a line of light around the edges, or, if you're lucky, a shadow. When I write, the same process takes place in my head: I'm looking into imaginary windows which I've devised for myself, and asking questions such as: who lives here? What's happening in their lives? What time of day is it? What season? Who, in particular, am I watching? Are there other people somewhere else in the story whom I should consider, or can I concentrate on this person? What sort of a story will it be? Most important of all: where am I going to situate *myself as the writer in relation to the people in my story*? It's as though I had a camera in my hand. What shall I focus on? Where will the edges of the picture come?

Occasionally the windows I look through are real, and I write stories about actual places, such as Lancaster Castle in *Billy's Hand* or a launderette near my house in *Letters of Fire* or my grandmother's flat in a forthcoming book called *My Grandmother's Stories*. Most of my work is not in the least autobiographical, but a great many of the settings are places I know, or can recall, and if I were to unpick each story and each novel, there would probably be quite a few autobiographical threads discernible here and there.

After looking in through real or metaphorical windows, we still have to decide to write about one thing rather than another. Most people write about their obsessions, the things which capture their imaginations, the ideas, thoughts, images which lodge in their minds and refuse to budge, no matter what. It's hard for a writer to say what these are, to make a list of them, but I can say this: it seems, from what I've written, that I like writing about:

a) old people in relationships with young ones;
b) families with lots of children (maybe because I am an only child);
c) the deceptive nature of physical reality;
d) exile and homelessness;

e) strong emotions, such as love and jealousy;
f) memory, and the way the past affects the present.

It also strikes me that I enjoy the details of food, setting, clothes, jewels, furniture and so on. Certainly I love describing them. I'm fascinated by sewing, knitting, embroidery, tapestry, and the silk, wool, needles, etc. which go with these crafts. Sometimes when I'm writing I have a strong sensation of stitching something together, and embellishing it, and (when things go wrong) unpicking bits of it. I think of a story as having a *fabric*, a textured surface. I imagine it being smooth or rough, and more or less ornately decorated. Two other things that I'm constantly intrigued by are photographs (particularly old ones) and mirrors. I'm also very fond of hair, and hair and mirrors play their part in the story called 'The Interview', which is included here.

'The Interview'—*How it developed*

a) One day, I sing the song 'I'm gonna wash that man right out of my hair,' and the thought occurs to me: what if you could do that? What if you could use a shampoo which would relieve the pain of breaking up with someone? What if you could FORGET them? What if you could forget ALL bad and unpleasant things?
b) At the hairdresser's, I think: we come here expecting transformations of a magical kind. We expect to change, to come out more beautiful, different, and we never do.
c) On Oxford Road in Manchester there's an old salon which has been boarded up and disused for more than twenty years, and I look at it every time I go into town. It's exactly as I describe it in the story.

These three things become twisted together into a kind of plait producing this idea: 'I shall write about a "magic" salon of some kind where you can go to rid yourself of unhappy memories.'

Decisions I made at first

a) This will be a matter-of-fact, first person story told from the point of view of a young girl working in the salon.
b) I will introduce 'magic' elements by using a lot of silvery words and images. The salon will have a silver door!
c) The owner of the salon will be glamorous, old, and wicked ... a cross between Cruella de Ville and Servelan in *Blake's Seven*. Smooth black hair in a tight bun.
d) Names are important. Pam (good, safe, honest) for the heroine and Madame Vilenska (overtones of Vilna in Poland, and 'vile', and general foreignness.)

As soon as I'd written ten pages or so, I knew it was wrong. The idea was too far-fetched, too unlikely for it to be done in this 'realistic' mode. The only way I could see to make it work was to stylize it. The first thing I did was get rid of the bustling, everyday salon and replace it with a mirror-lined room like an interrogation cell. Then I got rid of the whole supporting cast (Pam's mum, other assistants in the salon) and that left only Madame Vilenska and Pam, which I liked because it pared the whole thing down to a struggle between good and evil, with added pleasing contrasts between youth and age, and memory and oblivion. I chose to write the story with dialogue saying one thing and 'thoughts' saying another. It's not an original technique. Dorothy Parker has done it consummately well, but her story is sufficiently different in tone and outlook for me not to be worried about copying.

The colours in the story were important to me. I wanted only silver and black to contrast with the scarlet of Madame Vilenska's mouth and nails. I was all the time happily aware of associations with vampires and blood! I then added mauve/lilac for memories of a time when Madame Vilenska was young.

One other vital element came into the story after I'd started writing. I watched part of a film about the Holocaust called *Shoah*. What I saw was an interview with a barber whose task it was to cut the hair of those who were about to die in the gas chamber. As soon as I saw this, I recognized it as the last missing piece of a jigsaw. Of course, this was *why* Madame Vilenska was the kind of woman she was. This was her reason for being so terrified of memories. She had been just such a person, long ago, cutting hair at Auschwitz. This appears as *only one or two sentences* in the story: the reference to ashes and to hair falling on to stone floors. I expect no reader would even notice it if I didn't point it out, but it was important to me because it gave me an understanding of a character who would otherwise have been one-dimensional.

Finally, I was pleased with the ending. It's intended to produce what the French called a 'frisson'—a delicious sort of shiver. I hope it does.

Starting to write

When I know what I want to write about, even if it's only in a vague way, that's when the fun begins. First of all, I daydream about the story, turning it over and over in my mind while I peel the potatoes or push the Hoover about. This is pure pleasure, like playing a game of dolls' houses in my head, and if I'm not careful it can go on for months. There are some stories I've been playing with in this fashion for years. Decisions have to be made now. Whose point of view should I use to tell this story? Will it be in the first person (which is easier in some ways, but very limiting) or the third person? Even after I've decided, I may change my mind and have to rewrite chunks of prose or even the whole story, but I'm ready for this.

Next, I spend a pleasant hour or two making a rough plan which I may or may not follow, but which makes me feel safe, and also fosters the illusion that I am doing some kind of work. Then the day comes when you have to sit down, take the lid off your pen and BEGIN TO WRITE, and this is a terrifying moment. It's like diving into a swimming-pool, or like the first few seconds on stage before you speak, when every word you ever knew seems to have left your head. But (and it's important to remember this) *once the first sentence is written down the worst is over*. This is true even if what you have written is the purest rubbish and you're going to cross it out in ten minutes time. All the other technical problems you will encounter—and there'll be plenty—won't be anything like as bad because by then you will be *into* the process of writing, involved in it, anxious to communicate and above all wanting your story to become the one you've envisaged during your daydreams.

Who is the story for?

My novels and stories appear on the children's list. I write stories for very small children and also for what publishers call 'Young Adults.' Obviously, if I am writing something that I hope someone of five will like, I will not focus on the marital or financial difficulties in the life of a 55 year old tax inspector. It's only courtesy to your reader to write about what you think might interest them. But—and I would like to emphasize this—I don't regard writing for children as an easier option or in any way inferior to writing for grown-ups. I try occasionally to think of a suitable reply to the person who once asked me: 'Will you write a proper book when you've had the practice?' I was speechless at the time and still am. The main difference between children's books and 'grown-up' books is that the former generally (but not invariably) have children as the main characters.

It is true that when I'm writing a book for the 'Gazelle' series or the 'Cartwheel' series I think of who my readers might be. Beyond a certain level of understanding, though, (and I don't know at what biological age this takes place) I write to please myself. That sounds dreadfully selfish, but what I mean is: I try to write the kind of books I enjoy reading. I am, after all, the first person who has to be absorbed and interested, crying at all the sad bits and falling in love with the hero, and so on. When I've written the story and come to read it and correct it, and undo all the messy bits and do them again, then I think of Miss Godfray, Miss Sturgis and Miss Woodcock, who all taught me English. I look at what I've written through their eyes. Where would their red biros have fallen? Too many adjectives? Passages irrelevant to the main story? Two words where one will do? A complicated word where a simple one would be better? About all, I ask the question: what does it sound like? I read every word I ever write *aloud* and am amazed to discover that some people find this unnecessary. How they seek out clumsy rhythms and hideous repetitions is a mystery to me.

Language and style

A person's writing style is largely unconscious. All sorts of things (the way one was taught, the books one has read, the way one was spoken with as a child) go to create it, but it's almost impossible for a writer to analyse the elements of her own writing. There are, though, certain aims I have when I write, and the chief one is *to find a suitable language for the story I am telling*. Sometimes this will be direct, straightforward and conversational, usually in the first person. Sometimes I try for a more measured and, I hope, elegant and poetic style: slower and often in the third person. It depends on *who the people in the story are*. To put it at its most obvious: the language of a group of young soldiers in an army barracks will be different from the language of two old ladies in turn-of-the-century Cheltenham.

The setting, the time, the characters, the kind of story you're writing—all these *dictate* the language, and yet, oddly, I hardly have to think consciously about such things. It's almost as though, for each story, I put on a different costume and different kinds of words come out. I regard writing as another form of acting.

There are tricks that I enjoy using to create certain effects: jumping from the present to the past with flashbacks, alternating dialogue with narrative, starting at the end and working back to the beginning, experimenting in all sorts of ways. I don't find grammar or spelling a problem, but I am pedantic about some things. I would never split an infinitive or say anything other than 'different from.' I keep an eye on clichés and jargon and horrid expressions like 'at the end of the day'—unless, of course, it would be in character for one of the people in the story to use such words!

Rituals and reviews

I write everything lying on a sofa with a cushion behind my back. I write in Pentel on lined paper or sometimes in notebooks with beautiful covers. I'm crazy about stationery, and have many coloured pens and wonderful notelets, exercise books and postcards, and highly decorated files. I write very quickly (this essay has taken me about five hours, over two afternoons) but then I go back and read what I've written and cross out large chunks here and there. This hurts sometimes. I've just knocked out a splendid paragraph ... but it doesn't matter, it's gone. When you are given a certain number of words to play with, there's no space for fooling around. Once I've finished going over a story a few times, each time with a differently-coloured pen, the whole thing is a mess, and only I can read it. I then struggle up from the sofa to a typewriter or word-processor, and I type out my manuscript. Sometimes editors want a few tucks taken here and there: some things put in, others removed. This is what I call 'tinkering.' It's easily done on the word-processor, but there's nothing wrong with Sellotape and a pair of scissors. Sometimes editors are right, and I change the odd sentence or two, but sometimes I think I'm right and then I say: 'Sorry, but this stays as it is.' From time to time I write something and no one changes a word. That's lovely.

The editors of this book have asked us to include a bit of 'first draft,' but alas, I throw everything away the moment it's safely typed. I have kept one notebook which I take round to schools with me, so I shall include a page of what is, in fact, the first version of 'The Interview'. I will also send in the very messy draft of this essay.

After something is published, reviews of it may appear in the newspapers. I've been very lucky for the most part, but when someone doesn't like what you've written, it is, still, very much like being at school and being given what you consider to be a thoroughly undeserved bad mark ... and after having worked so hard too! Unfair, unfair! You have to tell yourself firmly that it's only one person's opinion, and that tomorrow someone will be wrapping this newspaper around some chips.

I have used up my word-ration. I will end with three bits of advice:

a) Keep it simple, but pay attention to detail.
b) Be honest, even when (especially when) making things up.
c) Read everything you write OUT LOUD.

THE INTERVIEW

Adèle Geras

Madame Vilenska thinks: They are all children and they understand nothing, nothing at all about what I am doing here. I am trying to create happiness and beauty in a world where little enough of it exists. Is that so wrong? Then tell me, someone, why I have been sitting here all day talking to one child after another, trying to find the one, the one who will comprehend me? I will press this . . . this buzzer . . . so . . . and yes, here is another one. Dark. Plain, but with possibilities . . . but then hasn't everyone the possibility of beauty? Isn't that the philosophy on which I have based my entire professional life? If not beauty, then glamour, chic, style, something. We can also change . . . oh, the bliss of metamorphosis . . . ducklings into swans . . . how marvellous.

Madame Vilenska says: 'Good morning, child. I'm so sorry to keep you waiting. Your name?'

'Pamela Duncan. My friends call me Pam.'

'And how old are you, Pam?' Madame Vilenska says the name, rolling it around in her mouth as though it were a plumstone, as though she is secretly looking for a place to spit it out.

'I'm nineteen.'

'And why have you applied for this job?'

'I've always wanted to be a hairdresser . . . ever since I was about six.'

Pam remembers a bus ride long ago. She and her mother on their way to town during the rush hour. They are stuck in a traffic jam, but she doesn't care. There is a row of boarded-up shops visible from the window. All the space is covered with posters. Pam has just learned to read and here is a patchwork quilt of words spread out in front of her, waiting to be said aloud. There are red and yellow and black words, printed in fat letters, or skinny ones, or uneven ones falling about all over the place. Normally such an abundance would keep Pam happily deciphering for long minutes, but then she notices something else: a line of tall, silver words right across the front of one of the closed-down shops. Pam reads them aloud to her mother:

' "Carroll Arden. Stylist to the Stars." What does that mean?'

Pam's mother says: 'That used to be a hairdresser's long ago. That's what stylist means. Hairdresser.'

'But why stars?' Pam wants to know.

'Stars means actresses or dancers. There were lots of threatres and music halls round here in the old days. I shouldn't think Carroll Arden did film stars . . . there can't have been too many of those. . . .'

Pam tastes the words, thinks of them for a long time. Stylist to the stars . . . it sounds beautiful to her still. Of course, these days, she knows exactly what stars are, but even so, when she says it to herself, an image of dark skies and whirling galaxies, of a million glittering silver pinpricks on a background like blue velvet comes into her mind.

'And what makes you think you have any talent in this area?' Madame Vilenska is suddenly fascinated, it seems, by her own hands. She stretches them out on the desk in front of her and appears to scrutinize them carefully: long, white fingers ending in glossy claws of nails painted the colour of aubergines. Madame Vilenska wears fingerless black lace gloves. She thinks: It is as though a black, scaly bark were growing over my skin . . . as though I were turning into a tree. . . . She shivers. Better to turn into a tree than have to look at the brown stains spreading themselves over the backs of my hands . . . age . . . there is nothing that anyone can do about it. I try. No one tries harder than I do. . . .

'I've always cut my mother's hair. And my sister's. All my friends get me to do their hair . . . you know . . . if there's a party, or anywhere special they have to go.'

'But there is more to this business than simply doing people's hair, is there not? Tell me five things . . . yes, five . . . that you think a hairdresser should try to achieve.'

Pam thinks: No one said there would be questions like this. She's a strange person, this Madame Vilenska. I can't decide whether she's beautiful or hideous. Perhaps she's both at the same time . . . *can* you be both at the same time? Her lips are too shiny. Her hair . . . her hair looks like black patent leather . . . tightly wound into a bun at the back of her neck . . . it must pull so on her forehead. And her hands . . . I like the fingerless gloves. Would they look good on me? Or stupid?

'Well,' Pam frowns.

'Never frown,' says Madame Vilenska. 'I do not permit frowning. Frowning makes wrinkles and I do not like wrinkles, therefore I do not allow frowning. Is that clear?'

'Yes, Madame.' Silly old bag, Pam thinks, you're not my boss yet, are you? You can't tell me what to do with my face . . . 'Five things . . . well, first, I suppose, you have to give the customer what she asked for, secondly, you have to make her look good, thirdly, you mustn't hurt her . . . with scissors or hot water or anything . . . and you must smile and make her feel you like her . . . I can't really think of anything else . . .' Pam's voice fades to silence.

'You are nearly right, but let me instruct you further. Most people, I have found, come here looking for two things: change and happiness. Women come here because they think that I can make them beautiful. They come because they are dissatisfied . . . with their hair, their skin . . . with their lives . . . with themselves. I offer them hope. Hope of beauty and happiness. I offer them transformations and metamorphoses . . . the possibility of love . . . a glimpse of paradise.'

Pam thinks: But the prices you ask! I saw them, up on the wall in the black and silver reception area . . . a glimpse of paradise for those with the right sort of income . . . what about ordinary women? What about my mum and my teachers, and the women I see every day on the buses, in the supermarket, in the street? No meta-what's it for them.

'I don't think,' says Pam, 'that most people come to the hairdresser's for happiness. Not really. I think they just want to make the best of themselves.'

'That,' says Madame Vilenska, 'is because you are young and innocent. But you will learn. Let me ask you something else now. What do you think are the reasons for human unhappiness?'

'Poverty, disease, war, famine ... pain ... unemployment ...'

'True ... all very true ... in a cosmic sense. But you ... tell me about yourself. Are you unhappy about anything?'

'Not at the moment ... no. I'm OK on the whole. Now.'

'Have you ever been unhappy? You are clearly a girl who has led a sheltered life ... but surely there must be something ...'

'Well ...'

'Don't be shy ... tell me ...'

Pam thinks: Her eyes are like a lizard's eyes: flat and black and I can't see where the iris ends and the pupil begins. Maybe she's hypnotising me ... some people can do that ... I know they can. I don't see why I should tell her everything. It's private ... but if I don't, she might ... I'll tell her a bit.

'There was this boy that I was going out with ...'

'Yes ... and did you love him?'

'Yes. People say you can't love anyone when you're fifteen ...'

'Then they,' says Madame Vilenska with the nearest thing to a smile Pam has yet seen, 'have never been fifteen.'

Madame Vilenska thinks: I have used my own treatments too well. All that's left to me is scraps: pale green trees ... and was there someone with dark brown eyes? I have a mauve blouse on ... it's hard ... so long ago ... but still, there's something left there ... a fluttering like a small bird trying out its wings ... what rubbish. All that is long gone. Gone with everything else.

Madame Vilenska says: 'Tell me about it. Go on.'

Pam says: 'There's nothing much to tell. He was a boy I met. At a party. We went out together for a bit and then I found out he was seeing someone else as well, and I asked him about it. He said it was true. He ... he liked this other girl better than me and so we broke up.' Pam looks at Madame Vilenska. 'It isn't anything unusual. It happens all the time. It happens to everyone.'

'Out of the mouths of babes and sucklings ...' says Madame Vilenska. 'It most certainly does happen to everyone. And did it cause you suffering? Pain?'

'Yes, of course.'

'And do the memories cause you suffering, too? The memories of that time?'

'I try not to think about it too much. I think about something else most of the time ...'

'But when you remember it, it hurts. Is that right?'

'Yes, it still hurts.'

Pam thinks: It was like being flayed, like having long strips of your skin torn away. Such hurt. You want to rub your eyes all the time, constantly. You want to erase it, crush it out of your brain, that picture that's outlined in black there, yes, there, right behind your forehead, branded into your consciousness: a picture of him doing the same things, saying the same things to someone else ...

'Well now,' Madame Vilenska says, 'let me tell you about the Oblivion Treatment. This is the reason, incidentally, that all applicants for this position have to be so carefully interviewed. I have to find precisely the right staff, otherwise the Treatment might be jeopardized.'

'But what is it, this treatment?' Pam asks. Oblivion means forgetfulness ... unconsciousness. She knows that.

'It is a skilful combination of hypnosis and certain very mild, non-addictive, oh, strictly non-addictive substances.'

'Do you mean drugs?' Pam says. 'I'm having nothing to do with anything like that.'

Madame Vilenska says: 'No, no, child. Not drugs ... goodness, no. Herbal infusions ... tisanes ... all strictly natural, growing things ... nothing artificial at all.'

And how lucky, Madame Vilenska thinks, that no one associates drugs with the scarlet tatters of the poppy, with the coca plant ...

'But what does this treatment do? Is it a beauty treatment?' Pam asks.

'The Treatment eliminates unhappiness.'

'That's marvellous,' Pam says. '*Can* you eliminate unhappiness?'

'Very easily.' Madame Vilenska nods. Again, Pam is reminded of a lizard ... such space between the eyes ...

'You eliminate unhappiness,' Madame Vilenska continues, 'by eradicating memories.'

'Unhappy memories?'

'Yes, of course.'

'But what about the others?'

'The others? I don't understand you.' Madame Vilenska never permits herself to frown, but she inclines her head to the left, to indicate bewilderment.

'The happy memories ...'

'I'm afraid they go also ... along with all the rest. Along with the unhappy ones. Most people do not have such a treasury of happy memories that they are unwilling to ... part with them.'

Pam says: 'Do people know? I mean ... is it allowed ... do people know that you do this? This Oblivion Treatment?'

'People?' Madame Vilenska smiles a little. Not too much. Smiling is nearly as hard on the face as frowning. 'Well, of course, my staff know. That is why I have to be so careful ... so discreet ... you understand, I'm sure. And one satisfied client passes the word to another, and so it goes ... word of mouth. The most powerful form of advertising in the world.'

Pam says: 'I'm afraid I have to go now.'

Madame Vilenska says: 'But why? Can you not see that what I am doing is for the best? Can you not see that there are those who are longing, begging me to take away the unbearable weight of their memories?'

Pam says: 'Maybe that's true ... but if you take *all* someone's memories away, you're turning her into a kind of ... I don't know ... a kind of zombie.'

'A zombie? Why? Why a zombie?'

'Because that's what a person is ... really when you get down to it ... a person *is* her memories. It's the memories, all of them, that make us all different. That make us who we are.'

'But it's memories that destroy us!' Madame Vilenska cries. 'I have blotted mine out totally. If it were not so, how could I have lived? After what I have seen . . .'

Madame Vilenska thinks: They are rubbed out. No longer there. As if I had taken the pictures and torn them across and across. Now they are tiny fragments, blown about in a strong wind . . . I catch a detail here and there. The rhythm of a train's wheels . . . the drifts of hair cut and cut and falling on the stone floor . . . smoke.

Pam says: 'That's all very well, but I want to remember everything. See it all, and feel it and remember it. Even if it hurts. I'm sorry.'

'I'm sorry too. You've led a very sheltered life. You would have made a good employee for Salon Vilenska. Never mind. I wish you every success in your career and I will press this buzzer and call in the next child . . .'

Pam thinks: Why is she staring like that? I can't see anything except her eyes . . . they are darker and darker now and wider and wider apart and I want to take my eyes away from those eyes and look at something else, but I can't . . . that's all there is . . . and I'm drowning in them, falling and falling . . .

Pam says: 'Thank you very much, Madame Vilenska,' and walks towards the door. A skilful arrangement of mirrows shows Madame Vilenska scores of Pams on their way out: out and up and on to the rainy pavements of the real world. She presses her buzzer, looks down at the black filigree of lace stretching over her hands, and waits for the next applicant to sit down.

* * *

'You didn't get the job, then?' says Shirley.

'No. I was offered it, mind,' says Pam. 'At least, I think I was. But I didn't want it.'

'Why ever not? Posh salon like that. I think there's something wrong with you. I do, honestly. Some of us would give our eye teeth for a job like that.'

'It was weird. She was weird.'

'Weird? How was she weird?'

Pam frowns. She says: 'I can't remember.'

PUBLICATIONS

Novels

The Girls in the Velvet Frame; Voyage; Happy Endings; all published by Hamish Hamilton

Collections of stories

Apricots at Midnight; Letters of Fire; The Green behind the Glass; My Grandmother's Stories; all published by Hamish Hamilton

Response

PLAYING THE WINDOW GAME

- What seems to be the motivation behind Adèle Geras's writing?
- What is the place of autobiography in her fiction? Think about other writers you have read whose work seems to be autobiographical. Discuss them with your group.
- 'Most people write about their obsessions, the things which capture their imaginations, the ideas, thoughts, images which lodge in their minds and refuse to budge, no matter what'. How does this statement compare with your own experience of writing?
- What are Adèle Geras's favoured topics in her fiction?
- 'Names are important', she writes. Think about other names in fiction that you have come across. Do you agree with Adèle Geras? What do certain names conjure up for you? Discuss this in small groups.
- Adèle Geras suggests that writing in the first person is 'easier in some ways, but very limiting'. What are your views on this? In what ways does using the first ('I') or third ('s/he') person narrator affect the narrative and what an author can achieve with it? Discuss some examples from your own recent reading.
- What differences and similarities does the author identify between writing for children and writing for adults? What are your own observations on books published for these supposedly different markets?
- Why does Adèle Geras recommend reading aloud what you have written? Do you think she's right?
- 'I regard writing as another form of acting'. What leads the author to make this statement?
- Look carefully at the draft page of her essay below. What changes and amendments did she make for the final version? Do you think the changes improve the text?

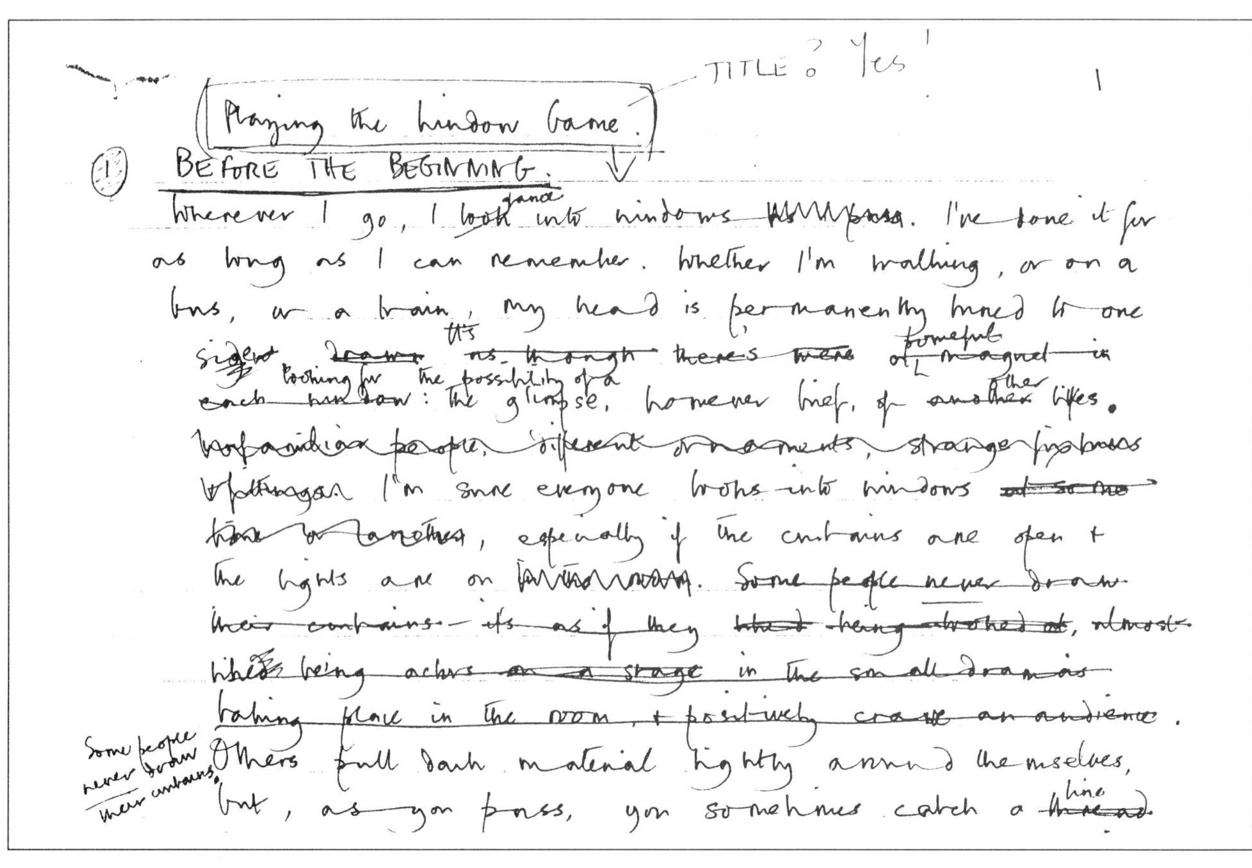

TITLE? Yes!

Playing the Window Game

(1) BEFORE THE BEGINNING

Wherever I go, I ~~look~~ glance into windows. I've done it for as long as I can remember. Whether I'm walking, or on a bus, or a train, my head is permanently turned to one side ... it's ... there's ... of powerful ~~magnet in each window~~ looking for the possibility of a glimpse, however brief, of ~~another~~ other lives.

I'm sure everyone looks into windows ... especially if the curtains are open + the lights are on. ~~Some people never draw their curtains – it's as if they ... almost ... being actors ... stage in the small dramas taking place in the room, + positively crave an audience.~~

Some people never draw their curtains.

Others pull dark material tightly around themselves, but, as you pass, you sometimes catch a ~~thread~~ line

THE INTERVIEW

- Adèle Geras comments in her essay that she enjoys having magic in her stories. How is the 'magical' element created and employed in 'The Interview'?

- 'Playing the Window Game' also emphasises the need for a 'suitable language' for any story. In what ways is Madame Vilenska's language, as shown in her thoughts and words, appropriate to the character and the story?

- Adèle Geras gives three tips to potential writers:
    1. Keep it simple, but pay attention to detail.
    2. Be honest.
    3. Read it out aloud.

  Does 'The Interview' follow this advice, and does it read well aloud?

- In the story we are given a closely-drawn picture of Madame Vilenska as 'glimpsed' through the eyes of Pamela. Look back over the narrative, paying special attention to clues about her past life and personality. Note down your impressions as follows:

Appearance	*Words*	*Thoughts*	*Actions*

Using the above notes, write a description of Madame Vilenska in the form of an entry in Pamela's diary, made soon after the story's events.

- Write a short commentary on the style of the story, and in particular its use of different narrators. What is achieved by the use of 'Pam thinks' and 'Madame Vilenska thinks'?

- Why does the story end the way it does? Rewrite the concluding paragraph to offer a different 'twist in the tale'. Does it produce for you 'what the French call a "frisson"' (page 16)?

- Look back to page 15 and the section on *How it developed*. Do you think the final story effectively blends together the author's original ideas?

- To what extent does 'The Interview' emerge as a story of contrasts—between good and evil, youth and age, memory and oblivion?

- What does the information about Madame Vilenska's background in Auschwitz add to your understanding and appreciation of the story? Should the writer have made the reference on page 23 more explicit?

- Would you class this story as belonging to the genre of crime or fantasy, or another genre altogether? Discuss this in your groups.

Fionnuala N. N' Hugh.

Fionnuala McHugh

LINES OF COMMUNICATION

Fionnuala McHugh was born in 1959. She went to the Loreto Convent in Omagh, Co Tyrone and read English at Girton College, Cambridge. She then studied law and as a member of Middle Temple was called to the Bar in 1982. In that year she was joint winner of the Vogue *Talent Contest for journalists. She has been a freelance feature writer since 1983. She writes for* The Times, The Mail on Sunday *and* Daily Mail, *and magazines* ELLE, Options *and* Country Homes & Interiors.

Journalism usually gets a bad press. That might read like a paradox but it's true. The only time journalists make the news themselves is when they've done something considered illegal—written a libellous article, for example, or infringed the Secrets Act—and when they've uncovered a scandal which most people are happy to read even as they're tut-tutting about the invasion of privacy. The general public, therefore, often thinks that a journalist is a man (still) with a foot in the door and a shifty expression in the eye. Those piggy-featured hacks you see propping up a Fleet Street bar in *Spitting Image* don't help matters.

The truth is that journalism is a term which covers all types of jobs and people. It can include television and radio broadcasters, book reviewers, sports commentators, magazine editors or reporters on local papers. I usually describe myself as a feature writer because contrary to what you might expect I've never written a news story in my life. I'm a freelance writer, contributing regularly to a selection of magazines and newspapers, and I've been doing it for five years.

I've never worked 'in house' on any publication, which is unusual and certainly wasn't intentional. Normally it's easier to spend a few years on a magazine or to work on a local paper before going freelance. When I was a graduate however, there simply weren't any jobs available. I wrote to all the women's magazines and they replied, with varying degrees of encouragement, that some experience was necessary. I wasn't even sure what I wanted to do when I was composing those letters. It's such a cliché, but I think I've wanted to write ever since I could hold a pen—and what you soon realise, even as an outsider, is that if you work on a publication you're liable to spend a lot of time commissioning other people to write, or thinking up headlines, or correcting somebody else's work. And the higher up you go, the further away you are from putting pen to paper. It's often one of the bizarre side effects of promotion in any job: you're usually removed from the arena in which you've proved yourself and need never use that skill again.

One night I wrote a feature about what it was like to be an Irish Convent girl arriving in England and I sent it to *Cosmopolitan* and they liked it. That was the only time I've ever written an article on the offchance that someone, somewhere will publish it and it just happened to be the kind of feature which *Cosmopolitan* likes. Since then, I've worked on a commissioned basis, for two reasons. First of all, I'm lazy—some features take a lot of research and expensive phone calls and effort. If I don't know at the outset that there's an interested (and fee-paying) party, I'd never get anything organised. Secondly, every single publication on the market prides itself on its individual style. The type of feature I write for the women's pages on *The Times* could never be transplanted onto the pages of *The Mail on Sunday* magazine. I need to know at the outset what kind of market will eventually end up reading what I've written. When I was studying English, both at school and university, I spent a lot of time comparing the styles of various novelists and playwrights, and in a way it's a continuation of that—you have to be able to adapt yourself accordingly.

That doesn't mean that you have to be a chameleon, because it's important to retain an identifiable thread in all writing. Often it's a question of differences in topic as much as in approach. *ELLE* and *Options* are both women's magazines. I wrote a feature about why young women decide to become nuns for *ELLE* a few years ago. It's unlikely that *Options* would run a feature like that because it's not relevant to their readers. I did an article on a slum in West Belfast for *The Sunday Times* : *The Mail on Sunday* magazine might find that too downbeat a topic.

Developing your own style, of course, is a horribly elusive process. It's like that useless command to a nervous party guest, Oh *just be yourself* ... I couldn't possibly define my style and I'm disconcerted if an editor makes some reference to it. It's like receiving a comment about a piece of clothing you didn't know you were wearing. In many ways I can't help feeling it's a bad thing to be over-analytical of one's own work: take it to pieces and it may never work again. This is partly as a result of being a freelance writer which increases neuroses and superstitions to an occasionally paralysing degree: I've often started to write something convinced that I'll never be able to reach a coherent conclusion.

Nevertheless I am aware of working to all sorts of internal rules. I think I must have had a particularly ferocious introduction to English grammar because to this day I think it looks untidy when a sentence finishes with a preposition and I'm very pedantic about the use of 'who' and 'whom'. I was given a copy of *Fowler's Modern English Usage* when I was a student, which I love reading, and Penguin's *Troublesome Words* is both entertaining and helpful. I loathe exclamation marks—if I could wipe them off subeditors' keyboards then I would. If something is exciting or funny then you should be able to make that clear without resorting to a vertical line with a dot underneath it. Emphatic underlining has to be used with caution and I never start a sentence with 'however'.

And although this essay is hardly a prime example, the word 'I' is often better left off the page. Writing in the first person is tricky in journalism. If you're doing a celebrity profile, it's liable to irritate the reader who wants to read what Kenneth Branagh, for instance, has to say and not the musings of A. Journalist. On the other hand you run the risk of appearing magisterial and aloof if you hand down anonymous judgement.

Profiles are a section apart even within the genre of feature writing. They're obviously more constrained than a 'think-piece' on, say, unemployment or capital punishment. What usually happens is that a celebrity has agreed to give an hour-long interview. He or she may be bored or disgruntled or nervous or jet-lagged. He or she will probably wish they were somewhere else and you may be the fifth journalist that morning to ask the same question. There's usually a promotion going on—of a film, a play, a book. I once had to interview Victoria Principal from *Dallas* for an hour in her hotel room. She had come to Britain to do a shampoo commercial and two representatives from the company sat in on the conversation. It seemed to be almost entirely about the condition of Victoria's hair. In the same week Britt Ekland came to London to promote a beauty book she'd written, and again each question—no matter what—was answered with reference to this book. In situations like that, you rapidly realise that nothing that you are ever going to say or do will break through such inflexibility so you simply have to ride with it and convey the problem in the subsequent article. It's the autopilot syndrome.

When I was growing up, I was taught that it was bad manners to talk about myself and polite to concentrate on everyone else. Funnily enough—and despite what I've just said about the written word 'I'—this rule doesn't always apply during interviews. The problem is that the situation is already an unreal one. There you are, usually in a hotel tea room, opposite an admittedly familiar face about whom you may have some press cuttings but no real knowledge, and in the space of an hour you are supposed to reach such a pitch of intimacy and perception that you can go away and write the definitive analysis of that person's character. It's an impossible task, of course. My worry is that nine time out of ten I like the person I'm interviewing. This could be for one of three reasons:

The celebrity is a hateful person but has learned how to handle the interview scenario to good advantage.

The celebrity is a hateful person but just happens to have hit it off with me today.

The celebrity is a nice person.

How does one know which is the truth? Phoning up some of the friends and working aquaintances of the celebrity is essential for an even faintly fair appraisal. As you progress in journalism this becomes easier because you're always meeting somebody who knows somebody else and theatrical people, for example, love to gossip about one another anonymously.

And you can try and have a decent conversation by giving your own opinions on something. The human response to the remark '*I* think that. . . .' is normally 'Well, *I* think that . . .' This is where a slightly devious and manipulative quality can come into an interviewing technique. If I make myself vulnerable to someone by expressing my innermost feeling about an emotional situation, that person is almost bound to respond in kind. But what I feel is irrelevant to the feature and doesn't appear in print: that other response is what matters.

The American writer Truman Capote once spent nine hours with Marlon Brando. For a while, he told Brando about his own problems and the difficult time he was having organising his life. Brando began to feel uncomfortable about this public display of vulnerability and offered some personal experiences of his own. These naturally formed the core of the published interview, to Brando's intense displeasure.

As I've never learnt shorthand, and notetaking can kill any pretence at normal conversation, a tape recorder is essential. It also fixes the tone of the conversation in one's memory. Think of a spoken sentence printed coldly upon the page, eg. 'Naturally I've always known where my talents lay.' Is that the voice of arrogance? Or irony? The retrospective matter-of-factness of old age? The optimism of youth? I could write down an entire conversation on a page and by slipping in either derogatory adverbs (glibly, smugly, falsely) or complimentary ones (sincerely, thoughtfully, helpfully) convey two entirely different impressions of the speaker. That is the power of words and the responsibility of their use is borne by the writer.

Beginning a piece is always difficult. If a first sentence feels wrong then the subsequent structure never loses that shakiness. I don't have a word processor. I always write in longhand, black pen on yellow paper (white is too paralysingly blank). I edit as I go along, trying to establish a rhythm. You could, in theory, keep on editing forever. How can you ever feel that a piece is perfect? I've never written a feature and thought—Yes, that's exactly what I wanted to convey. Words are evasive: they slide out of your grasp just as you're ready to pin them onto the page. But sometimes a sentence construction gives a momentary tingle of rightness—and that's what you spend the rest of your time trying to recapture.

Usually the words that I strike out when I'm editing a piece go because they're redundant. Repetition is inevitable when you're writing against a deadline. It's irritating when you see a feature in print and realise that the same word has appeared three times in as many sentences. And editing often involves untangling complicated sentences or arguments. Very few people speak with absolute coherence. They'll hop about all over the place trying to impress the force of their arguments upon you, the journalist. If you transcribed their speech *verbatim*, no reader would ever reach the end of the feature. Not only are you editing your own words, you're also editing someone else's without distorting the sense of what they said. Veracity of course is the boundary within which the journalist—unlike the playwright, the novelist, the poet—has to work. The other writers are bound by form, the journalist by content.

As an example of self-editing, this is how I worked out the first few sentences of the Kenneth Branagh profile which follows:

Kenneth Branagh looks ~~very~~ slightly weary. ~~Sometimes his voice trails off~~ He/constantly runs ~~his~~ nailbitten fingers through /his thick, reddish-blond hair as if to /re gather his thoughts into coherence, but ~~stillhis voice occasionally~~ sometimes his voice trails off, distracted by other ~~pressures~~ concerns. Over ~~constant~~ coffee in London's Riverside Studios, he is handed ~~a sheaf~~ sheaves of messages, he is called away to the phone. These are the pressures of running your own ~~theatrical~~ company—the Renaissance Theatre Company—which Branagh founded with fellow actor David Parfitt earlier this year.

I wanted to convey a physical sense of an actor exhausted by his commitments, and by juggling words both to elicit the reader's sympathy and to explain why this man was so tired. I wanted to emphasise but not by repetition, and I also wanted to give a sense of rhythm to the opening paragraph which would set the tone for me as much as for the reader.

Whether I eventually achieved this I don't know. I have no idea what the reader thinks by the time he or she finishes a piece I've written. Because I'm writing this essay, you'll presume a certain level of competence and confidence in me which I won't feel is justified. Every single commission is a challenge over which I can never be sure I'll triumph. Being freelance, in particular, has all the insecurities of acting: you are only as good as the last article you wrote. All the time there's a self-questioning: can I express this better? Is that the right phrase? Am I being fair and impartial? Can the language I use accurately convey the thoughts and actions of another person?

Two things keep me going amidst the self-doubt. The first is reading the words of other people. The stimulation to be had from good writing, whether in magazines, newspapers or books, can hardly be over-emphasised.

And the second thing, which is the basis of it all, is a love of language. I can't imagine doing anything else. Even when it's 2 a.m. and every word I know seems to have shrivelled up and died in my brain and the yellow paper looks whitely bare, some line of communication wants to remain open. That's what I have to cling to because, after all, that's what writing is about.

Options: November 1987

PROFILE: KENNETH BRANAGH

Fionnuala McHugh

He describes himself as Mr Bloody Average, yet in acting circles he's known as the Young Olivier. In fact he's 26, Northern Irish and something of a phenomenon.

Kenneth Branagh looks slightly weary. He constantly runs nail-bitten fingers through his thick, reddish-blond hair as if to re-gather his thoughts into coherence, but sometimes his voice trails off, distracted by other concerns. Over coffee in London's Riverside studios, he is handed sheaves of messages, he is called to the phone. These are the pressures of running your own company—the Renaissance Theatre Company—which Branagh founded with fellow actor David Parfitt earlier this year. Their first play, *Public Enemy*, was written by Branagh, starred Branagh and was produced by him. Later this month he directs Richard Briers in *Twelfth Night*; next spring he will play Hamlet. In the meantime, he has just finished filming *Strange Interlude* with Glenda Jackson.

Not once throughout the afternoon, however, does he show impatience at being interviewed or photographed. At 26, his courtesy appears to have already become his trademark in theatrical circles. 'What's so extraordinary,' says one actor, 'is that nobody wishes him ill. People don't want him to fail.'

Despite his high turnover of work, the chances are that you will not have heard of Kenneth Branagh. His main output has been in the theatre, most notably with the RSC, which while earning him the respect of critics and peers has not brought him public recognition. On television, apart from an adaptation of D. H. Lawrence's *The Boy in the Bush*, his biggest role has been as Billy in the BBC's adaptation of Graham Reid's quartet of plays set in contemporary Belfast. He is currently starring in the BBC's seven-part serial, *Fortunes of War*, adapted from Olivia Manning's *Balkan* and *Levant Trilogies*. He also has a starring role in the film *A Month in the Country*. As a result, people may soon begin to recognise him on the street, though as a critic once remarked, the reason no one pesters Branagh on the Tube is because he looks too nice and normal to be an actor. Branagh himself thinks it entirely unreasonable that anyone should be expected to know who he is. 'I'm one of those soufflé actors,' he grins, 'ever rising.'

The rise, in professional achievements, has been swift. It's only five years since he left RADA, but in his final term he had already started filming the first of the Billy plays, *Too Late to Talk to Billy*. When he went for his audition, there was initial doubt about his ability to provide the requisite Northern Irish accent. To everyone's relief (and surprise) it transpired that Branagh had been born, like Billy, in Protestant, working-class Belfast and had only emigrated to England in 1970, when he was nine. His father, who makes ceilings and partitions, was working over here fairly frequently, the Troubles were gearing themselves up into full-blown strife and a move had seemed wise. The family (parents, older brother and then new-born sister) settled in Reading. Branagh attended what he called a 'rough and tumble comprehensive' and became involved in the dramatic society. 'Now that interest seems to have been there all the time, which is surprising, given my background, but I always used to remember the names of stars or the make-up artists—any names—at the end of every programme or film.'

As is often the case, there was an encouraging English teacher, one Stanley Brew, in the background. 'He was a great enthusiast, he made you not afraid to relish writers and books. And history, I loved—I loved the personal dramas, the huge moments of human folly.'

He seems never to have doubted his inclination to try for a place at RADA. His parents, though they didn't attempt to dissuade him, were concerned that he would have nothing else to fall back on in case of failure. At a recent performance of one of his son's plays, Mr Branagh Sr was heard asking another actor, 'Do you really think Ken's got a chance in this business?'

The young Branagh, convinced about what he wanted to do though not about his ability to do it, worried about life in London; about the risks of unemployment; about socialising with other actors. 'I thought all actors were a certain kind of predatory, dressing-gown-wearing character...' And his upbringing in that no-man's land of Northern Ireland accentuated this apartness.

He still feels 'betwixt and between' in his nationality. 'I can't deny certain aspects of my personality, which are distinctly un-English. There's a particular brand of fire—I'm not suggesting that the English aren't fiery—but the Celtic variety exists in me as opposed to the English sort. There's a certain slightly mad, romantic streak, or something ... when I got back there, I feel it more, I feel part of it and yet I'm away from it.' His accent now is regionless, classless—a bit, as he says, like the world of acting, where actors are 'slightly floating creatures'. But he pinned himself into the initial role of Billy with great success, and his reappearances in the series have come at suitable punctuation points in his progression. He turned down the role of Judd in the film *Another Country* (a part for which he had won both the SWET and the Plays and Players Best Newcomer Awards in the stage version) so that he could make the third Billy play. He is, points out one actor, renowned for his loyalty to the other members of his profession.

It is this loyalty which is partly responsible for the existence of the Renaissance Theatre Company. Branagh and Parfitt worked together in *Another Country* and subsequently co-produced minor lunch-time events and works connected with the 'Not the RSC' festival. A sufficient rapport was established to mount a co-production of *Romeo and Juliet* at the Lyric Studio in Hammersmith last summer. Branagh financed the cost of the production with money from his work on the film *High Season*. 'The commercial management wouldn't do that,' one of the actors involved recalls. 'It couldn't make a profit because of the size of the auditorium, although it had full houses every night, and Ken lost money. But he created work for 11 actors, two stage managers and the technical crew.'

Branagh is wary about being slotted into the hero's role in this, however, although he's far too honest (and tired) to pretend that it's been easy. 'David has more appetite for it than I do, but it's necessary to do my share. It's difficult putting on shows, budgeting; difficult doing all those bits actors normally don't think about. David's pretty unflappable, but I get a bit ... anxious. Sometimes I feel I'd just like to run away; I get scared.' He believes a guilt-ridden and puritanical streak has pushed him into this endeavour, that he isn't worthy of the offers which drop easily into his lap. 'I suppose I could—though I never believe it—but I *suppose* I could, after the RSC and the few bits I've done, have waited for the next film or telly series to come along. I never assume that will happen. I'm always amazed when people ask me to do things, which sound stupid and coy but I bet most actors are the same. I suppose I have an extra reaction against any kind of complacency.'

The title Renaissance is intended to reflect both the notions of a reawakening and an era in which talent was less rigidly pigeon-holed. The company hopes to encourage others to expand their arts-related capabilities: for example, next spring Geraldine McEwan, Judi Dench and Derek Jacobi will direct *As You Like It, Much Ado About Nothing* and *Hamlet* respectively.

'I'd quite like to dispel the notion that to do more than one thing is somehow an indication of spreading yourself too thinly or burning yourself out,' Branagh says. Hence, the incentive to write *Public Enemy*, which first appeared on paper in a splurge of enthusiasm two years ago. He wanted to write about Belfast and the effects of long-term unemployment, and the process was equally exciting and terrifying. 'It's a bit like acting. If I'm on at eight o'clock, at five to eight I'll be thinking, "Why do I do this, why do I do this?" But as soon as the curtain goes up I'll think, "I do this because this is where I'm at the centre of myself." And the same with writing the play—the prospect of doing it was an Everest, but once I got going I enjoyed it enormously.'

He wants to write more—another play, perhaps a novel. 'I wish to be someone who occasionally has something they want to say, which I believe is a proper extension of one's work as an actor—if that's my central contribution as an artist.' A slight pause ... 'Phrases like that are so pretentious, aren't they?' A horror for such pretension or insecurity permeates his conversation. When he talks about the standards he sets himself, he does so apologetically. ('This is a bit heavy, isn't it?') And he's aware of the pressures which may, even in his unique position as producer-cum-actor-cum-director-cum-writer, dissipate such ideals. 'It's very hard to do and talk about without setting yourself up to sound like a saint.'

He has grown tougher in what is a tough business, however. He finds that he can cope with bad notices better than he'd ever thought possible in earlier, more sensitive days. 'There's a quote from Chekhov's letters which I looked up once when I was reeling from one notice. Chekhov said art, especially the stage, is an area where it's impossible to walk without stumbling, where you go through wholly unsuccessful days and, indeed, seasons where you're vilified, disappointed and have misunderstandings and terrible anxieties. But you must accept that and fanatically and continually go your own way. And I think he's right. If you didn't you'd be even more miserably unhappy.'

People he admires—Olivier and Gielgud, of course, Anthony Hopkins, Judi Dench ('She moves about six and a half inches off the stage for me') and Derek Jacobi—have had such necessary commitment to their careers. 'And Woody Allen's another. He has that dogged pursuit, he follows his own way. It's all in their blood; they can't *not* do what they do.'

As for his own sense of purpose: 'Yes, I am in the middle of what I want to do. Even when you're in the grip of a panic, when a bit of you loathes the drama of it, there is that bit of you which enjoys it.'

In some ways, his position is a difficult one. He has received critical acclaim (The Young Olivier is the frequent label), he now has his production company, he is about to play Hamlet, he has tasted film and television. Tempting offers assail him at the moment: to write, to act, perhaps to direct. 'I really don't know what's going to happen,' he admits. 'Last night I was offered something for next year which would take up a couple of years of my life. It's very exciting but it's forcing me to think about what I want to do.'

He has considered taking a university course. 'What I lack is a more extensive and expressive system of thought. I don't know . . . you run out of words.' He laughs. 'The Hamletian streak is quite strong in me at the moment.' This is not, he says, a sign of dissatisfaction with his current lifestyle—more like 'immense curiosity'.

There are negative aspects to all this. 'There isn't enough time for *life* at the moment. I can't see me working like this for ever; I can't. I have to keep it in perspective. I'm doing exactly what I want and that's a luxury.' He lives alone in a south London flat, which he bought nearly three years ago. When he first moved in he was desperate for a base after months of roaming from room to room. Now he says that if Renaissance needed money he would not think twice about selling the flat.

Personal relationships are hard to maintain, 'I have to resolve that within myself. In a very minor way, you can see the costs you allow yourself to pay. But I just think this is an extraordinary time for me. And I *wouldn't* be happy if I was married with two kids.'

He describes himself as Mr Bloody Average. 'In fact, I keep thinking, "Christ, why aren't you going on benders or something?" You know, like all those Finneys and O'Tooles. I don't do anything extraordinary. I think: "Why don't I go to night-clubs or something?" But I don't fit in with that soft of stuff.' He grins wryly, tiredly. He recognises that every second of his time is accounted for. He accepts the areas of sacrifice.

'His talent and charm are limitless,' says one of his friends. 'You know you're working with someone touched by genius.'

Response

LINES OF COMMUNICATION

- What are your reactions to Fionnuala McHugh's comments in her opening paragraph? What is your view of journalists and their profession?

- What two reasons does Fionnuala McHugh give for working on a 'commissioned basis'?

- What does the journalist mean about her job and writing when she says that you don't have to be 'a chameleon'.

- What does Fionnuala McHugh say about her style of writing and the importance of 'internal rules of language? Do you agree with her views?

- 'You run the risk of appearing magisterial and aloof if you hand down anonymous judgement'. What tensions of style is the journalist talking about here? Compare her views with those of Adèle Geras in the context of writing fiction.

- In what ways are 'Profiles' different from other kinds of feature writing, according to this journalist? What particular difficulties are encountered in compiling a 'Profile'?

- 'It's the autopilot syndrome'. What does the writer mean in this sentence?

- 'Phoning up some of the friends and working acquaintances of the celebrity is essential for an even faintly fair appraisal'. Is this prying too much? Do you feel that famous people have to accept everything that is written about them? Discuss this topic in groups.

- How does the journalist succeed in finding out about someone's innermost feelings? Would you trust being interviewed in this way by a journalist?

- In what ways is a tape-recorder helpful to the interviewer?

- 'Veracity of course is the boundary within which the journalist—unlike the playwright, the novelist, the poet—has to work. The other writers are bound by form, the journalist by content'. What does Fionnuala McHugh mean here? What implications are there in what she says in connection with *editing* an interviewee's words?

- Compare the draft first paragraph on page 29 with the final version on page 31. Do you feel the journalist succeeds in her intention 'to convey a physical sense of an actor exhausted by his commitments'?

- In what ways is freelance writing rather like acting, according to this journalist?

PROFILE: KENNETH BRANAGH

- What impressions do you think the sub-editor wished to convey to the reader through the title/introduction?

- 'Kenneth Branagh looks slightly weary'. Why does the Journalist begin with these words? What effect does a short sentence have on the reader?

- From the opening paragraph what sort of picture do you have of the actor?

- Why should an actor comment that 'People don't want him to fail'? What does this perhaps tell us about the theatrical world generally?

- According to Kenneth Branagh's early experience, what are the risks of the acting profession?

- From your reading, what effect does being brought up in Belfast seem to have had on the actor?

- 'Art is an area where it's impossible to walk without stumbling'. What does this tell us about the forces which motivate artists, and this actor in particular?

- 'The Hamletian streak is quite strong in me at the moment'. What does he mean by this? Research into the character of Shakespeare's hero.

- Looking back over the article, are there aspects of Kenneth Branagh's character that the journalist seems to want to emphasise? Give some examples.

- What evidence is there that the journalist has talked about the actor with other people in order to write a fair appraisal of him?

- Write a 300 word description of Kenneth Branagh for:
  a) *Who's Who*
  b) A theatre programme
  c) A teenage magazine

  Remember your different audience in each case, and match your style to the publication.

Berlie Doherty

GRAN—AN ADAPTATION FOR TELEVISION

I was brought up in the Wirral and now live in Sheffield. I have been writing for about nine years, and my books for children include How Green You Are, The Making of Fingers Finnigan *and* Children of Winter, *which have been televised on Jackanory,* White Peak Farm, *which has also been serialised on Children's BBC TV,* Tough Luck, Spellhorn, Tilly Mint and the Dodo, Paddywack and Cosy *and* Granny Was a Buffer Girl, *which was awarded the Carnegie Medal in 1987.*

I enjoy reading and singing, and walking on the Derbyshire hills.

'Gran' is the first episode of a three-part television series, *White Peak Farm*, based on my novel of the same name. If anyone had asked me a couple of years ago if I would be interested in writing for television I would have said no. The medium is so different from novel or from radio-play writing, I wouldn't have known where to start. I couldn't see how you could begin to tell a story through visual images and without the use of descriptive language.

Luckily for me I was invited to script my own drama series, and having my own novel to write from gave me a good start. I knew the story and its characters and I had a strong imaginary sense of its setting.

So, in a way, my task was a technical one. I had to think first about reducing a novel of nine story-chapters in to a drama series of three episodes, each of which had to be self-contained and satisfying as a one-off play, but which had to have a strong linking theme with each of the other two episodes.

The book, *White Peak Farm*, is about a family who have lived on a farm for generations. My starting point was to wonder what would happen if the members of that close-knit community began to separate and go their own ways in life, for whatever reasons. What kind of a threat would this be to the farm and to the family? Because it is a novel about people I decided to focus the three episodes of the drama series on three groups in the family, and to show how their lives and the decisions they made about them would affect the central character, teenaged Jeannie. The three groups are: Gran; Kathleen and Martin (Jeannie's brother and sister); and Madge and John (her parents). Episode One, 'Gran', introduced the disturbed relationships between Kathleen and her father which will, in a later episode, lead to her leaving home. It also dropped clues about Martin, and the fact that farming isn't his most passionate interest in life, as his father would wish.

Throughout the novel there is a narrator, Jeannie, who is always observing, always absorbing the changes that are taking place in the farm and her family, and ultimately in herself. Her 'voice' in the book and in the play is important, and the first thing I needed to do in both was to establish that voice. In the novel it's a kind of literary voice, as if she's writing her thoughts down for the reader. In the television play it's a more natural voice; she's actually speaking to you, the viewer. You might like to consider the tone and the language of these two openers, where Jeannie is saying the same thing in different ways:

NOVEL

My home is on a farm in the soft folding hills of Derbyshire. Not far from us the dark peaks of the Pennines rise up in to the ridge that's called the spine of England. We've always lived there; my father's family has owned the farm for generations. He never wants to let it go.

PLAY

JEANNIE V/O (VOICE OVER):
My home is on a farm, among the hills. We've always live here. My dad's family has owned the farm for generations. I can't imagine living anywhere else, or wanting to see anything but these fields, and these hills, with all their changing colours . . .

You will see in the text that my instructions or directions to the producer take the place of the kind of visual description we might expect to find on the page of a novel, where our imagination creates the pictures. Of course I can't expect the sheep or the clouds to behave in the way I suggest, but these directions help the producer to establish the right sort of atmosphere, just as the introduction of music helps the viewer.

In the next phase of the introduction the arrangement of ideas differs. The opening paragraph of a novel, just like the opening shots of a film, are like a shop window, telling you a lot about the kind of things you might expect to find in the shop when you go in. Here the objects on display are slightly different:

NOVEL

Nothing ever seemed to change there. The seasons printed their different patterns on the fields, the sky cast its different lights across the moors, but our lives, I thought, would never change. Mum, Dad, Kathleen, Martin, Marion and I; Aunt Jessie and Gran. And yet, about four years ago that change did come to us, casting its different lights across the pattern of our lives. I suppose it all started with Gran.

PLAY

I live in a house of secrets. There are things going on that I don't understand, changes that are happening that no-one will talk to me about. Sometimes I feel as if I don't know my family any more. Dad, Mum, Kathleen, Martin, Marion. They've all got their secrets. Even Kathleen. She's my sister but she's always been my friend too. But even she keeps things from me now. We used to share everything. Now she won't tell me anything.

In the novel the character on display in that first chapter is Gran, and we move very quickly to meet her and to find out more about her. In the television play, the whole family is in focus to start with, and Jeannie's relationship with Kathleen, which is soon to become very distant, has to be established before we meet Gran and follow her story. You may be interested to know that in the actual television play the entire section inside Gran's cottage (scenes 5, 6 and 7) had to be cut because the play was over-running by several minutes. Do you think it made any difference that it was cut? What do you think I was trying to establish in those scenes?

The birthday party scene (9) is important because we see all the family together for the first time, but also we see the beginnings of what Jeannie had hinted at earlier on: 'Changes that are happening that no-one will talk to me about.' This web of security which is the family is beginning to disintegrate.

The next scenes dovetail into one another as a series of clues about why Gran is leaving, and also about Jeannie's feeling of hopelessness about the inevitability of it. But at the same time other things are going on because the viewer has to be aware that Gran's isn't the only story to be followed, so we have clues about the way Kathleen's behaviour is alienating her from John (Boy-mad, that's you!') and about the relationship between John and Martin ('White Peak Farm will be yours one day, you know. When I'm good and ready mind, not before.').

The next time we see the whole family together is in scene 15. It's important at this point to re-establish the closeness of the family, so we have a warm scene of story-telling by firelight, letting the camera create the atmosphere before any dialogue starts. But all this closeness will be destroyed by John's intrusive anger—a hint that he, by his own nature, is playing a large part in the destruction of his own farm and family. The scene also brings us back to the main theme of this play—Gran's leaving.

From now on the scenes drive towards that point with the preparation for the farewell party and the selling of Gran's cottage. The key scene of the play is not the last one, but scene 22. Here Gran and Jeannie's special closeness is established. This is where they really say goodbye to each other, and where Jeannie faces that frightening and exciting moment in her own life when she is aware that her childhood is behind her and that ahead of her is the unknown landscape of her future. 'Promise me that, Jeannie,' Gran says, 'that you won't waste your life.'

Here the visual effects of television helped to show in a few seconds what had taken a couple of pages to describe in the novel. They are standing on a bridge, and that symbolises the point they have both reached in their lives. The rush of water below them is the energy of Jeannie's life, the hope that will carry her through Gran's leaving and through all the things that will happen on her farm.

At the beginning of the essay I described the process of dramatising a story as being technical. I hope you see that it is also creative, because the camera establishes atmosphere and helps us to describe. If you try to adapt a story for television you must guide the camera to use it to its best advantage. It's not simply a case of lifting out the dialogue from a story. If an action can be shown it doesn't need to be talked about. You can reduce the dialogue of a scene (a short story is made up of scenes, too) or do without it altogether. Sometimes, as with Jeannie's narration, you may want to change the tone to make it more immediate. Sometimes you may have to develop or insert dialogue so that one scene moves smoothly into another. You may have to change the order of events (as I did by bringing Kathleen into scene 3) because you feel all the characters need to be introduced more quickly.

I think one of the most important lessons I learnt was to trust the camera. If the camera can say it, the characters don't need to. But you, as writer of the script, have to tell the camera what to look at. In scene 24 the camera is Jeannie and Jeannie is you, observing something very private and important, and it is a scene without any words at all apart from the murmuring of the women. Here television is feeding our imagination, not doing all the work, and I think that matters too. Whatever the medium, the most important thing is the link between the imaginations of the writer and of the reader or viewer.

PUBLICATIONS

Children of Winter, 1985; *Granny Was a Buffer Girl,* 1986; *How Green You Are!,* 1982; *The Making of Fingers Finnigan,* 1983; *Tilly Mint Tales,* 1984; *White Peak Farm,* 1984.

All published by Methuen.

WHITE PEAK FARM: GRAN

Berlie Doherty

EPISODE ONE: GRAN

SCENE 1: ESTABLISH WHITE PEAK FARM *[Introductory music*

A deep-sided valley scape, focusing down to a neat sheep farm on a hillside; a hill farm. A girl (Jeannie) is sitting with her back to us on a dry stone wall. We hear a tractor coming across a field. A man (John) is driving it. He jumps out and bales hay from the back of it into the trough the sheep eat from. He watches the sheep approach. They nose against each other, eating from the trough; their cries are audible.

JEANNIE (V/O) My home is on a farm, among the hills. We've always lived here. My dad's family has owned the farm for generations. I can't imagine living anywhere else, or wanting to see anything but these fields, and these hills, with all their changing colours . . .

We see, as if we are the girl, the colours of far and near hills shifting in sunlight, and cloud shadows racing across the fields.

[Music contd.

SCENE 2: THE FARMYARD *[Music contd.*

The tractor comes down towards the farmyard where a woman (Madge) is flinging grain for the hens. A lad (Martin) is sweeping out the lambing shed which is close to the farmhouse. He looks up when he hears the tractor. As the tractor approaches, a little girl (Marion) runs to open the gate for it. She stands on the gate and allows it to swing her back. As the tractor passes through her father shouts at her to get down.

[Music contd.

SCENE 3: THE LANE BY THE WALL *[Music contd.*

An older girl (Kathleen) comes down the lane trotting Beauty, the farm horse. As if she's been waiting for her, Jeannie slips off the wall and goes to meet her. Kathleen reins in the horse and they walk together towards the house, Kathleen still on Beauty. They're laughing together. All this during Voice Over:

JEANNIE (V/O) I live in a house of secrets. There are things going on that I don't understand, changes that are happening that no-one will talk to me about. Sometimes I feel as if I don't know my family any more. Dad, Mum, Kathleen, Martin, Marion. They've all got their secrets. Even Kathleen. She's my sister but she's always been my friend, too. But even she keeps things from me now. We used to share everything. Now she won't tell me anything.

[*Lyrical climax to music, and fade out.*

JEANNIE Where've you been, Kathleen?

KATHLEEN Oh ... over the hills and far away. Actually I've been getting Marion's birthday present. [*She grins wickedly, expecting Jeannie to accuse her of lying.*]

JEANNIE I've got her some felt pens. I wish we had another horse.

KATHLEEN Why?

JEANNIE Well, then I could have gone with you.

KATHLEEN Sometimes I think you've got no imagination, Jeannie.

[*It suddenly dawns on Jeannie.*]

JEANNIE Kathleen. Have you got a boyfriend?

[*Kathleen pretends she hasn't heard her.*]

JEANNIE Have you? You have, haven't you?

[*Kathleen whistles tunelessly, then bursts into giggles.*]

JEANNIE Tell me who it is then.

KATHLEEN Who who is? [*She bursts out laughing again.*] Hoo-hoo-hoo-hoo-hoo is?

JEANNIE Go on. Or I'll tell Dad.

[*Suddenly serious, Kathleen swings round on her. Her laughter turns to anger and then to unhappiness.*]

KATHLEEN Don't you dare, Jeannie Tanner. Or I'll run away and I'll never come home again. And it'll be your fault.

[*Jeannie is alarmed and bewildered at Kathleen's words. Madge's voice breaks their locked stare.*]

MADGE Jeannie! Your Gran's going. Walk down with her, will you?

SCENE 4: EXT. GRAN'S COTTAGE

Jeannie and Gran walk down to the door of Gran's cottage and stand together talking. Gran points up to the swallows swooping to come together on a telegraph wire.

GRAN Time for leaving, Jeannie. Always a sad time, when there's a leaving in the air.

[*Jeannie registers this, not quite sure what Gran is telling her.*]

GRAN (CONTD.) Are you coming in for a little? Don't have to get straight back do you?

As they go in we glance back with Jeannie to see the swallows and, below them, autumn leaves drifting down from branches.

SCENE 5: INT. SITTING ROOM, GRAN'S COTTAGE

It is an old cottage with heavy old-fashioned furniture. A big stone ewer in the hearth is filled with autumn flowers, gold chrysanthemums, and these give the room its warmth. There's a chest in a dark corner and on that there's a white conch and a photograph of a man in a World War II uniform. There are no other ornaments. Jeannie loves to come here. She likes to sink into the deep armchair by the window and look out up to the hills. She does this when she comes in. Gran hangs her coat behind the door.

GRAN You've time for a quick cup, before you do your farm jobs?
[*Gran laughs at the face Jeannie pulls because she knows that farm jobs are a chore to Jeannie, and that she'd much rather stay with her. When Gran goes out of the room, Jeannie gazes round it, loving it. She kneels in front of the chest and holds the shell to her ear. She kneels back, cradling the shell. Noticing the chest as she has done many times, but this time, taking courage to ask about it.*]

JEANNIE Gran?

GRAN Yes?
[*Jeannie goes to kitchen.*]

SCENE 6: INT. KITCHEN, GRAN'S COTTAGE

JEANNIE [*Coming in to kitchen*] Gran. What's in that chest?

GRAN Oh, you'll find out one day, Jeannie. What's in there will be yours, one day.

JEANNIE Mine? But what is it?

GRAN You'll see. [*She is deciding how much to tell Jeannie*] A long time ago, Jeannie, I went to University. Did you know that?

JEANNIE [*Absently*] I think so, Gran.

GRAN Well, it was very unusual in those days for village people to go to University. It was nearly unheard of for girls to go. But I went, you see. They were all very proud of me, round here. I was only a girl. A shy girl. Like you. [*She picks up the tea tray.*]

JEANNIE What was it like, leaving home? Were you scared?

GRAN Oh yes. Very. But I was proud, too. I was doing something I really wanted to do. The most important thing in my life. [*Pause*] But I'd only been at Oxford a year when I had to come back home again. My mother had been taken ill, you see, and needed nursing. That was a daughter's job. So . . . That was the end of that. [*They go back to the sitting room.*]

SCENE 7: INT. SITTING ROOM, GRAN'S COTTAGE

Gran and Jeannie enter.

GRAN ... And a couple of years later I was married.

JEANNIE I can't make Kathleen out these days. One minute she's happy, and the next she's crying. It doesn't make sense.

GRAN What d'you think it might be?

JEANNIE I think she might be in love.

GRAN Of course she is. But it's never easy, you know. You'll find out for yourself one day. Poor Kathleen. She's cultivating for herself an inevitable sadness.

SCENE 8: INT. GIRLS' BEDROOM. MOONLIGHT

Kathleen is crying into her pillow. Jeannie lying in bed watching her.

JEANNIE Why are you crying?

KATHLEEN Don't ask me, Jeannie.

JEANNIE (V/O) Gran knows what it is and she won't tell me, any more than Kathleen will.

SCENE 9: INT. THE FARMHOUSE

The birthday tea. All the family are round the table. The candles are lit on the cake, and Marion is leaning forward to blow them out. All singing: 'Happy birthday to you.'

MADGE Come on, Marion. Big blow, now.
[*Laughter and cheers as Marion succeeds in blowing out the candles. Gran cuts into the merriment as Madge stands up to help Marion cut the cake.*]

GRAN Madge, I'm thinking of selling my house. How much should I ask for it?
[*Madge, astonished, stands with the knife still poised. She can't believe this.*]

MADGE You're selling your house? Whatever for?

GRAN I'm moving.

KATHLEEN Where to, Gran?

JOHN Don't be ridiculous, Mother. What's the point of moving?

MADGE And what about all your furniture?

GRAN I've no need of that, not where I'm going.
[*John and Madge exchange glances.*]

MARTIN Are you moving in with us?

JOHN What do you want to sell your house for anyway, at your age?

GRAN Because I need the money...
[*Marion is upset because she's lost everyone's attention. Kathleen tries to chivvy the birthday along.*]

KATHLEEN Come on Mum. Let Marion cut her cake.

[*Impatient, John pushes his plate away from him. Madge supports Marion's hand while she cuts the cake, but she is watching her mother and her husband. John pulls back the curtains.*]

JOHN If you're short of money you've only to ask, Mother. You should know that.

MADGE I think we've a right to know why you want to sell your house, Mum. And where you're thinking of going when you have sold it.

[*Marion is troubled by her mother's tone, and also by the fact that her birthday seems to be passing by unnoticed.*]

MARION Mummy? Can't I cut it? It's my birthday cake.

MADGE Yes, love. Do it now. Try and persuade your Gran to have a piece.

GRAN I've made plans. I've held them in my head for over fifty years. I'm not going to change my mind now.

JOHN If you're going to get all secretive about it, I'm off. I've better things to do outside. There's a sick ewe to be seen to in the old barn.

[*Marion is trying to cut the cake, to prevent the party breaking up.*]

GRAN My intentions are to go travelling.

JOHN Travelling! At your age!

GRAN I should have thought there was more good reason to go travelling at my age than at any other.

[*They all slump into silence. Marion passes the cake round, John refuses a slice. He goes over to the porch to put his boots on. Jeannie and Gran sit where they always do. Near the window. Looking out at the great flank of hill that thrusts away from the farm. Gran's thoughts seem far away.*]

JEANNIE Where d'you think you'll go, Gran?

GRAN Oh, a long way, Jeannie. And when I get there I am going to stay.

JEANNIE Forever?

[*Gran doesn't answer. She's looking at the hills.*]

JEANNIE But where?

GRAN Maybe ... it'll be somewhere like India.

[*She says this softly, as if she's revealing a dream. Having made her impression, Gran is not prepared to say any more. She stands up and takes her coat down from the hook, buttoning it up decisively.*]

JOHN India! But you've never even been out of this country, Mother! It's ten years since you last went to town!

GRAN Exactly. Thank you for the tea. Will you walk me home, Jeannie?

SCENE 10: EXT. THE LANE

Jeannie and Gran walk down the lane together.

JEANNIE Gran. You're not really going away, are you?

GRAN Yes, Jeannie. I am.

[*Jeannie is puzzled, but accepts it as yet another secret that's being kept from her.*]

SCENE 11: INT. FARM KITCHEN

There's a log fire. Marion, forgotten, is arranging her birthday cards. Martin is at the table with her, drawing her a card. It's as if the conversation has been going round and round.

JOHN India! Why India of all places?

MADGE Land of poverty.

[*Martin looks up from his drawing, which Marion takes from him to show her mother.*]

MARTIN Land of mystics.

MARION Look, Mummy! Martin's drawn me a birthday sheep!

[*Madge takes the card and looks at it absently.*]

MADGE Bed now, Marion. Off you go.

MARION But Mum! It's still my birthday.

JOHN Now, your mother said.

KATHLEEN I'll take her up...

[*Kathleen doesn't want John's temper to spoil Marion's birthday. Marion unwillingly kisses her mother and starts up the stairs. Kathleen, following her, remembers.*]

KATHLEEN Mum. Remember the slide show the Vicar gave us...

MADGE I do. That talk about the Himalayas...

KATHLEEN That's it ... he told us about people who went out to India as doctors and nurses and teachers. Don't you remember? He said we all had it in us to make that sort of sacrifice.

[*John, about to go out at last, wrenches his jacket down from its hook by the door.*]

JOHN What sort of sacrifice! The man's mad! Wait till I see him.

SCENE 12: EXT. LANE FROM THE FARM

The lane is muddy. John is on the horse Beauty, blustering, and the vicar is delicate in soft shoes on the path below him. John's temper is up, and he has little respect for this man.

JOHN Shame on you, Mr. Curry, for putting wild ideas into an old lady's head.

VICAR Ah! She's told you. I wanted to have a word with you.

[*The vicar and John are at odds, as the vicar knows nothing of the explanation Gran has given the family. Being a gentle, patient man, he suffers John's anger and understands it to be grief.*]

JOHN We'll not hear of it. We're not going to let her go.

VICAR I've made good provision for her. I've done exactly what she asked me to do. You must trust me, Mr. Tanner.

JOHN Trust you! Expecting an old lady to make that sort of sacrifice!

VICAR But it's the only sort of sacrifice the old can make. It makes up, don't you see, for being old . . .

[*John Tanner doesn't want to see. He swings his horse round till her rump is inches away from the vicar's face. Then canters away with a huge spattering of mud.*]

SCENE 13: EXT. THE LANE. LATE AFTERNOON

Jeannie and Marion have been dropped by the school bus, and come up the lane together.

MARION There's Martin, look. He's been rabbiting.

[*Martin is whistling up the lane behind them, a couple of dead rabbits slung over his shoulder, and a sack. As he comes up to them he tosses the rabbits over to Marion, who tries to dodge away from then, half-scared, half laughing.*]

MARTIN Here y'are, Marion.

MARION I don't want them!

MARTIN Take them in to Mum. For tonight's stewpot, tell her.

[*Marion runs off towards the house holding the dead rabbits well away from herself. Martin unwraps the sack he's been holding and takes out his ferret, which he pours from hand to hand, knowing it distresses Jeannie. She watches him, disliking him.*]

JEANNIE I hate that ferret.

MARTIN Nothing to be scared of.

JEANNIE I'm not scared of it. I hate it. I hate you, when you're like that. Killing rabbits with it.

[*He looks across at her, mocking, laughing, cruel.*]

JEANNIE You look just like Dad.

[*Martin holds back the ferret's face out to her, pulling its mouth back in a fierce snap.*]

JEANNIE I don't understand you. You can sit for hours drawing animals and birds and things, and the next minute you can go out and kill them, just like that. You enjoy killing them, don't you?

MARTIN Foxing's even better. I've seen a fox snap a dog's jaws off, as soon as look at him.

JEANNIE I suppose you think that's fun, Martin Tanner.

MARTIN It's neither fun nor cruel. It's nature, that's all.

[*He scoops the ferret up and swings it into a bag. We are aware of how like his father he is, and how hard it is for Jeannie to feel close to him, her only brother. They continue up the lane. Kathleen comes through a gate, waves and waits for them. She looks happy, having just come from her boyfriend. She's wearing make-up and has her hair loose.*]

MARTIN Does my Dad know you've been out looking like that?

KATHLEEN Looking like what?

[*Martin laughs. He's fond of this sister but he likes to make fun of her.*]

MARTIN A city tart.

[*Kathleen stares at him, insolent, waiting for him to go and leave her alone. He laughs and swings himself up on to a wall, watching her, still cradling and looping his ferret. Jeannie and Kathleen turn themselves away from him, so they're looking in on the camp-site in the field. There are a couple of tents. For a few moments we, and they, forget about Martin.*]

JEANNIE Where have you been?

[*Kathleen shrugs, smiles to herself, lies.*]

KATHLEEN Gran's.

JEANNIE Isn't there anything we can do to stop her?

KATHLEEN Why?

JEANNIE I don't want her to go.

KATHLEEN That's not the point, is it?

[*Jeannie doesn't understand Kathleen. They hear their father coming. Jeannie takes Beauty's reins as he swings down.*]

JOHN I might have known you two would be lounging around here. There's work in the house you know, and on the farm.

[*The girls exchange glances. It's as if their father only notices them to tell them off.*]

KATHLEEN We were just talking about Gran.

JOHN I know very well what you were just doing. You were watching out for lads in those tents, that's what you were doing.

KATHLEEN I wasn't, Dad.

JOHN Boy-mad, that's you. I've watched you. Get off home and help your mother.

[*There's a cruel sort of mockery in his face when he says this. He knows he's hurting her, and that his grievance isn't to do with her at all. Kathleen is too hurt to look at Jeannie. As she runs off John shouts at her.*]

JOHN You can get that muck off your face, too.

[*He sighs. He's fed up with girls. Jeannie wants to be with him and, thinking his next speech is to her, stays. Martin puts his ferret back in the bag and swings down to join them.*]

JOHN If I had my way there wouldn't be tents on this field. There'd be sheep, that's what farm-land's for.

MARTIN You should never have sold it, Dad.

JEANNIE Was this our field?

JOHN What else could I have done, Martin? You tell me what else could I have done? Boy Baxter!

JEANNIE What did Boy Baxter do?

JOHN Never you mind what Boy Baxter did. He's a bad farmer and a bad neighbour. That's all you need to know.

JEANNIE Why do you hate him so much?

[*John shakes his head, irritated by her question.*]

JEANNIE I thought he had a good farm.

JOHN What d'you know about farming! Anyway, I've done what I could to keep this farm going. Got it looking grand again. (*To Martin*) It'll be yours one day, you know.

[*Martin laughs. He and his father often share these lines, deadly serious even though they joke.*]

JOHN When I'm good and ready, mind. Not before. See to Beauty will you? And check the top field for me.

[Jeannie takes the reins, upset because once again she has been pushed out by Martin. Martin and John walk off together, away from the farmhouse, friends as well as father and son. They've forgotten Jeannie. She nuzzles the horse. She watches them go, then swings herself up on Beauty's back. Kathleen has just come out of the house in her wellies and catches her up. Jeannie reins up.]

JEANNIE Kath! Come up top field.

[She helps Kathleen to pull up behind her. Laughing, as if this is something they haven't done for ages, the two girls set off at a trot.]

SCENE 14: EXT. TOP FIELD

Jeannie and Kathleen galloping, laughing, on Beauty.

KATHLEEN (*Shouts*) Whohoo!

[They follow the walls, sometimes checking the gates or stiles. Way above the farm they slow down and Kathleen slides down. Jeannie joins her. Allowing Beauty to crop the grass near them, they lean against a wall, looking at the farm which is far below them.]

JEANNIE Dad's a pig to you, Kathleen. I don't know why he said that to you.

KATHLEEN I do. He's scared of losing us.

JEANNIE Us? He couldn't care less about us girls.

KATHLEEN He's scared of anything happening to White Peak Farm.

JEANNIE Why should it?

KATHLEEN It's everything to him, this farm.

JEANNIE But why should anything happen to it?

[Kathleen is distressed, she finds it difficult to express the way she's feeling.]

JEANNIE Is it something to do with Boy Baxter?

KATHLEEN Could be. Don't ask me about him ...

[She knows more than she's willing to share.]

JEANNIE Why won't anyone tell me about the Baxters?

KATHLEEN It's something that happened a long time ago. When you were little.

[Jeannie knows this isn't all, but that she'll have to be satisfied. We see the farm far below, its lights coming on for the evening.]

JEANNIE I can't imagine living anywhere else, can you? But it's never going to be the same now, is it? Not if Gran leaves us.

SCENE 15: INT. FARM KITCHEN: EVENING

Gran and Marion are sitting together by the fire, firelight playing on their faces. Madge is ironing sheets. As Jeannie and Kathleen come in, Gran is telling stories to Marion, who is leaning against her, sucking her thumb. We have a sense that Kathleen and Jeannie are bringing the cold in with them, as Gran shifts a little to make room for them near the fire. Jeannie squeezes on to the settee, Kathleen sits on the hearthrug, Gran doesn't stop her story, however, and soon Jeannie and Kathleen are absorbed in it.

GRAN ... I used to go in to the city when I was a little girl, your age, Marion. I used to go in with my mother. Oh, I hate cities.

JEANNIE Me too!

GRAN Ah! You're like me, Jeannie ... Kathleen's the city girl.

[She means that Jeannie is a country girl too. They understand each other. John has come in, stamping his boots off in the porch. Martin leans against the porch behind him.]

KATHLEEN I can't see what you hate about cities, Jeannie. I love going into town.

[John shouts across at her. He's angry and tired. He has to take it out on someone.]

JOHN That's all you do care about. That's what you'll turn out to be—a city tart with painted fingernails and coloured hair. That's you.

[Martin laughs, catching his father's eye to share this taunt, though John isn't laughing. Kathleen is burning with hurt and embarrassment. Gran leans forward to touch her, to show she's sorry, but Kathleen shakes her off. Madge, resigned to this, sighs and takes the iron to the sink to cool.]

MADGE You're a bit hard on her, John.

JOHN It's for her own good. She knows what I mean.

[Kathleen, eyes smarting, swings herself round so her back is to the family. She lifts the logs in the fire with a poker and we watch the flames burst as Gran says quietly:]

GRAN Well, I'm going to ask Kathleen to make a trip into town for me, and Jeannie with her. I want to have a party, Madge, before I leave. The girls can buy the food for me.

[Jeannie suddenly knows that Gran really will leave them. Gran puts her hand over hers, and we see their hands. The feeling isn't sentimental, but supportive. Gran is willing Jeannie to be strong.]

GRAN I've no intention of sneaking away without a good send-off, I might as well warn you now. Though I've never given a party before. But everyone will be invited to this one. Except, of course, Boy Baxter's family.

[Gran gives Kathleen a strange sideways look, which causes Kathleen some embarrassment. Jeannie is puzzled, wondering what Gran could have found out that she didn't know.]

MARION Can I go with them?

GRAN I'd rather hoped you'd stay and help me pack, Marion. I might have one or two little presents to sort out, too. It's going to be a busy day for all of us ...

SCENE 16: EXT. BUS STATION, NEWCASTLE

Jeannie and Kathleen jump down from the bus. Trying to hide their giggles they crouch over the shopping list. They can hardly speak for laughing. Everything seems ridiculous to them.

KATHLEEN What have we got to get, then? Crabs!

JEANNIE I've never seen a crab. Dead or alive.

KATHLEEN Fresh, she's written. How can you tell if a crab's fresh?

JEANNIE I suppose they'll all be walking around the stall. Waving their arms at us!

SCENE 17: INT. MARKET

There are crabs moving slightly on a fishmonger's slab.

JEANNIE What did I tell you?

KATHLEEN She's got them tied to a bit of nylon thread on her thumb. Look at that! [*The girls are still giggling. Jeannie holds out a carrier bag as stallholder tips crabs into it. Kathleen groans and turns away, sickened.*]

KATHLEEN Ugh—I think I'm allergic to crabmeat.

JEANNIE But you haven't tasted them yet. [*Stallholder watches Kathleen.*]

STALLHOLDER Can't stand crabmeat myself. Makes me retch, every time. It's the cleaning of 'em. You can empty your insides out if it's not cleaned right.

SCENE 18: EXT. GRAN'S COTTAGE

'Sold' sign. Gran comes out of the door with Madge, goes to the gate, looks back, and climbs into the waiting tractor. John is loading some of her furniture onto the trailer. Marion is there too.

SCENE 19: EXT. BAKER'S SHOP

The girls come out clutching sticks of french bread.

KATHLEEN We'll probably all get food poisoning with these crabs.

JEANNIE Perhaps that's what Gran wants.

KATHLEEN What d'you mean?

JEANNIE If she has changed her mind about going to India. She could say the crab had made her ill and then she'd have to miss her plane.

KATHLEEN Not even Gran could be that devious.

SCENE 20: INT. THE FARM KITCHEN

Gran is rummaging in a carrier bag. Marion runs to her and kneels down, excited, knowing that Gran has something for her. John carries Gran's chair in and puts it by the window.

JOHN Here you are, Mother. Your old armchair. You might as well have a bit of comfort before you set off on those travels of yours.

GRAN Here, Marion, this is what I'm looking for.

[*Gran brings out her conch shell.*]

GRAN This is for you to keep forever. My shell that sings of the sea. Listen!

[*Marion nods, delighted, intent on listening.*]

GRAN Not that we've been to the seaside, any of us. Where's Kathleen, then?

KATHLEEN I'm here, Gran.

[*Kathleen comes in, followed slowly by Jeannie. Kathleen goes to Gran to take the bag she is giving her. Gran whispers to her.*]

GRAN For Kathleen, the City Girl!

[*There are some rings in the bag. Kathleen bends down to hug Gran and stays with her head on Gran's shoulder. Gran pats her back.*]

GRAN Now then, who's left? Martin!

[*She laughs and Kathleen straightens up and moves away from her to show Jeannie the rings. Gran gives Martin a carriage clock.*]

GRAN Look after it, Martin. It's yours now.

[*Martin, pleased, embarrassed, doesn't know what to say. He tries to joke.*]

MARTIN Does it work?

GRAN Sometimes. It's a bit like me.

[*They are all relieved to laugh.*]

MARION Where's Jeannie's present?

GRAN Jeannie knows what her present is. Your father's taken it up to your room, Jeannie.

SCENE 21: THE GIRLS' BEDROOM

Kathleen and Jeannie follow Marion into the room. The chest has been put by the window. Jeannie goes straight to it, kneels by it.

MARION What's in it?

JEANNIE I don't know.

KATHLEEN Open it then.

[*Jeannie lifts up the lid.*]

MARION Books!

KATHLEEN What a rotten present, Jeannie. You can share my rings. Not the moonstone one though.

[*Kathleen goes—but Jeannie delves down into the box and brings the books out. She opens a leather bound copy of Wordsworth. The name inside reads: Annie Burton, Oxford, 1938. Jeannie closes the book and hugs it to herself.*]

•

SCENE 22: EXT. RIVER

We hear Gran's voice as we watch a stream tumbling its way down the hillside. Sense of the hills' grandeur.

GRAN Are you pleased with your present, Jeannie?

JEANNIE Oh, I am! I'll always treasure them. [*Kisses her*] Gran ... I wish you weren't going.

GRAN I should be quite at home in India you know, Jeannie. They have mountains there too.

[*Gran and Jeannie are leaning against a small stone bridge. They look tiny till we draw into them.*]

JEANNIE But why so far, Gran? And why forever?

GRAN People think they know what's best for you, and they don't. D'you know that, Jeannie? The only harm you can do to yourself is to waste your life, and you can do that if you don't listen to your own voice. That's a terrible crime, to waste your own life.

[*Gran leans against the bridge with her back to it looking up at the hills, speaking softly and calmly. Jeannie isn't looking at her but at the river, so although she's standing next to Gran she's leaning forward against the bridge.*]

JEANNIE D'you think you've wasted your life?

GRAN I know I have. It's a terrible thing to come to my age and to say that. And you don't even know it's happening until it's too late. Not if you're listening to other people instead of to yourself. Don't let it happen to you, eh? Promise me that, Jeannie. That you won't waste your life.

SCENE 23: INT. THE GIRLS' BEDROOM. NIGHT TIME

Jeannie is lying awake.

JEANNIE (V/O) And I did promise her. But how can I keep a promise like that, that's what I'd like to know? I felt as if I was saying goodbye to Gran then.

[*She is aware of a murmur of voices upstairs. She slides out of bed and creeps past her sleeping sisters.*]

SCENE 24: STAIRS AND ATTIC ROOM, SEEN FROM STAIRS

Jeannie creeps up the attic stairs. There's a light on in the upstairs room. Jeannie sits on the top step. Madge is sitting on the bed in Gran's room, talking softly to her mother. As Gran struggles to sit up she takes her hand. Gran's hair is loose and her nightie looks too big for her. Madge settles Gran down again and strokes her hair as if she was a child. All this is seen from the stairs. Jeannie goes back to her own room.

SCENE 25: INT. THE GIRLS' BEDROOM AS BEFORE [*Moonlight*

Jeannie creeps close to Kathleen's bed.

JEANNIE Kathleen. Are you awake?

[*Kathleen stirs slightly, as if she hadn't been sleeping.*]

JEANNIE Mum's upstairs with Gran. She's just sitting on her bed, holding her hand. Kath ... I think Gran's crying.

[*Kathleen sits up slowly, rubbing sleep from her eyes. Jeannie sits on her bed.*]

JEANNIE I've never noticed how thin she's gone, had you? She looked just like a little girl crying in the night because she's scared. Just as if she wanted her own mum to comfort her.

KATHLEEN Could you hear what they were saying?

[Jeannie is unsure whether she's heard properly, or whether she wants to share it with Kathleen yet.]

JEANNIE I think so. . . .

SCENE 26: EXT. FARMYARD

Trestles have been set in the yard. The family and guests are seated and eating. The talk is lively enough, though Jeannie is watching Gran. Gran holds out a plate of crab to her.

GRAN This crab really is very nice, Jeannie. Won't you have some?

JEANNIE No thanks, Gran.

GRAN No? Kathleen?

[Kathleen shakes her head. The talk is louder, there is much laughter. John bangs the table and stands to make a speech.]

JOHN I'm not going to say much. We've not always seen eye to eye, Madge's mother and me. Wouldn't be natural if we did. But I've a lot to thank her for. I think she made my Madge the way she is, a cut above the rest, I'd say.

[Madge looks up at him, surprised, laughing.]

JOHN So this is it. I wish you well, Mother.

[While the others lift their glasses he sits down abruptly, surprised by his own emotions. We see the faces of the listening guests and family one by one. Gran stands up. She is confident and happy, and the listeners take their mood from her.]

GRAN I'm having a lovely time at my party. That's what I want to say. And it's a darned sight better than being at your own funeral. D'you know why? Because you can listen to all the nice things people say about you, and still tuck into all the grub . . .

[Laughter. Madge stands up, holding up her glass.]

MADGE To Gran!

[The toast is echoed with raised glasses.]

SCENE 27: INT. THE GIRLS' BEDROOM

Jeannie has gone up to her room and opens a window. She sits on the sill, watching the activity outside, and seeing Gran asleep under a tree. She sees and hears the vicar's car. She is looking at one of Gran's books.

SCENE 28: EXT. THE FARMYARD

Marion jumps off the gate and runs to open it.

MARION He's here!
[*Old Morris car comes up the lane.*]

SCENE 29: INT. FARMHOUSE KITCHEN

Kathleen wipes her hands on tea towel and flings it across the sink as she hurries out.

SCENE 30: INT. GIRLS' BEDROOM

Jeannie closes her window.

SCENE 31: EXT. FARMYARD

Madge goes to stand by Gran, who is still asleep. Mr. Curry gets out of the Morris. Martin brings Gran's case into the yard and puts it by the car. Madge touches Gran's shoulder.

MADGE Mum! Wake up, Mum! It's time . . .
[*Gran jumps up, bright, and kisses them all lightly. Like her they act without fuss. Mr. Curry puts her case into the boot and holds the door open for her. Gran steps in, waving and smiling. The family cluster round the car. Gran and Jeannie exchange calm special glances. Jeannie says nothing, while the rest of the family call:*]

FAMILY Bye, Gran. Bye!
[*Marion runs alongside the car for a bit, waving, then drops back. Car goes down lane. Gran looks back at bend, still waving. Car in distance, Gran's hand is a white speck. The family, hands raised and still waving. Jeannie turns to look at them one by one: John puts his hand on Madge's shoulder, Marion slips her hands into Kathleen's: Martin hangs his head.*]

[*Freeze frame*

JEANNIE (V/O) And I saw that the game is over at last, and that there isn't one of us who doesn't know by now that Gran isn't heading for India, or for anywhere abroad for that matter, but for the little hospice just outside town . . . where the incurably sick go to die.

Jeannie is brave, only just holding tears back, proud of Gran, not wanting to let her down now. Behind her the frame unfreezes, the family turn to go back in. Madge waits in the doorway for her, and as credits go up, Jeannie follows them in. Farm, tiny among hills, car a toy speck. Closes with flight of migrating birds.

Response

'GRAN'—AN ADAPTATION FOR TELEVISION

- What reasons does Berlie Doherty give as to why it is difficult to turn a novel into a television script?

- Take up Berlie Doherty's invitation on page 37. Consider the tone and the language of the two 'openers', one from the novel, the second from the playscript. What similarities and differences do you notice?

- Looking at the extracts on page 37, in what ways do the arrangement of ideas differ? Look carefully at the vocabulary used by the writer.

- 'The process of dramatising a story . . . is both technical and creative'. In what ways can television work much more effectively and quickly than the written words, according to Berlie Doherty? In groups, discuss examples of books or plays which you have read that have been dramatised for film or television. What have been the gains and losses from the page to the screen, in your opinion?

- 'Whatever the medium the most important thing is the link between the imagination of the writer and of the reader or viewer'. Discuss this statement in groups. Write an essay arguing your point of view on the topic.

- Does televison often over-feed our imaginations? Debate this subject in your groups.

WHITE PEAK FARM: 'GRAN'

- What does the writer try to do in scenes 1–3? How does she use the technical aspects of television to achieve her goals? Look closely at the directions as well as what the characters say.

- Look again at scenes 5–7. What is the writer wishing to establish here for the viewer? She tells us that they were cut eventually because the play was over-running. What has been lost?

- Write a character description of Jeannie based on what she says, what she does, and on what others say about her. What do you think Berlie Doherty thinks of her?

- 'The only harm you can do to yourself is to waste your life, and you can do that if you don't listen to your own voice. That's a terrible crime . . .' (page 52). What does Gran mean here? Why does she say this to Jeannie?

- At the end of Scene 31 the writer uses 'Freeze frame'. Why? Where else in the play might it be appropriate to use this television technique?

- At what point in the play did you realise that Gran's plans to go to India were a cover-up for her leaving for a hospice? Look back over the text to see what clues there are.

- 'Episode One introduces the disturbed relationship between Kathleen and her father', writes the author. Look for examples of this relationship in 'Gran'.

- What clues are revealed about Martin's character? For example, the writer tells us that 'farming isn't his most passionate interest'.

- 'In the television play the whole family is in focus to start with, and Jeannie's relationship with Kathleen has to be established before we meet Gran and follow her story' (page 38). How successful is Berlie Doherty in doing this in your opinion?

- Scene 9 is important, according to the writer. In what ways does this scene work, and how is it vital to the narrative?

- Scenes 15 and 22 are also key ones, according to the writer. Discuss them in groups. Are they successful television? How could they be improved? Do they work dramatically in relation to other parts of the episode?

- 'If you try to adapt a story for television you must guide the camera, to use it to its best advantage. It's not simply a case of lifting out the dialogue from a story. If an action can be *shown* it doesn't need to be talked about'. How successful do you think Berlie Doherty is in her dramatisation?

- Berlie Doherty indicates that radio and television scripts are very different. Rewrite a sequence of scenes from this play as a radio script. Remember your audience hears and listens! There are further notes for guidance on page 90.

Joan Lingard

OTHER WORLDS

Joan Lingard is the author of ten novels for adults and 18 for young people. She was born in Edinburgh but lived in Belfast from two to 18. She has three grown up daughters and lives now in Edinburgh with her Canadian husband.

I began to write when I was eleven years old and living in Belfast. I was a book addict, devouring them by the yard, haunting my rather scabby local library almost daily, but never satisfied. One day when I had nothing to read and was moaning in my mother's ear in the way that eleven year olds are adept at doing, she turned round and said to me, 'Why don't you write a book of your own?' Why not indeed? So I sat down with lined foolscap paper, filled my fountain pen with green ink (a suitable colour for a writer, I considered) and began the story of a girl called Gail who had fabulous adventures in Cornish caves, eventually bringing a band of fiendish smugglers to justice. Shades of Enid Blyton, you might think, and you would be right. I hope that, since then, I have shaken off her influence.

When I wrote that book I had never been to Cornwall, except in my imagination. Everything that I wrote in my early teens was set in places I had never visited. Not a word did I write about Belfast. Dull deadly old Belfast? Surely not the setting for exciting fiction! It was only when I came into my twenties that I realised I would write with more authority and therefore more convincingly if I wrote about places and people that I knew and understood. And so it seems to have been. I have set much of my work in Belfast and in Edinburgh where I was born and now live. This does not mean, however, that I write autobiographical novels. I use autobiographical material—backgrounds, incidents that have happened to me and other people, events, memories, fragments of overheard speech—but I take it and transmute it into the stuff of fiction. This means that I select what is relevant and reshape it. Real life is chaotic. Art attempts to bring order to that chaos and give it a form.

From the day that I sat down to write my first book I wanted to be a novelist, and nothing else, although for some years I did write quite a number of television scripts and recently have come to enjoy writing short stories as well. The short story requires you to be economical, to get off the ground quickly, to bring your characters sharply into focus and to eschew (avoid) sub-plots. The novel allows for greater complexity: there is more time and space to explore characters and situations in depth and breadth, and this tends to make for a richer tapestry. I enjoy the short story and the novel in different moods, but ultimately I will always plump for the latter.

When I start to read or to write a novel, I feel as if I am being sucked into another world; I enter into the skins of the characters. When I wrote my 'Maggie' quartet I felt as though I *were* Maggie, a feeling enhanced by using the first person, as I do in my short story *A Head For Figures*. There I am Seb—it doesn't matter that he's male and I'm female. I wrote first of all a short story entitled *Silver Linings*, told also in the first person but through the eyes of Sam, his sister. When I'd finished it I became curious about Seb and in the end wrote twelve stories about them, six from his point of view and six from hers, and they made a book called *Rags and Riches*, which could either be viewed as a collection of short stories or an episodic novel. I often find that my work builds up in this way, one idea leading to another. It is important to have reflective times to allow the ideas to surface.

For some weeks before beginning on a new novel, while still working on the final editing of the current one, I start a notebook. I jot down ideas, names for my new set of characters, snatches of conversation, short scenes. I might write the beginning, or the end. Then, when the current book has finally been sent off to the publisher, I block out, roughly, the structure of my next one, even though I know that I may diverge from it once I begin to write. I would hate to feel that everything was fixed and there was nothing to discover. I also decide what my time sequence will be and what season of the year I shall set the novel in. The mood I need to create might determine this, as for example, in *The Winter Visitor*, where I wanted to have a strange man arrive in a seaside resort out of season. If he had come in the summer his arrival would have passed unremarked and aroused no curiosity.

There are a number of decisions to be taken and for me one of the first is always the point of view. I like to know where my story will be centred. Shall I tell it from the point of view of one person, and if so, shall I use the first or the third person? The former has the advantage of immediacy, of taking the reader straight in; the latter of allowing you to see round the corners more. With the first person you have to limit your knowledge to what that character knows, but in spite of that restriction, or perhaps even because of it, I find it enjoyable to use. It would not always be suitable, however, and there are times when one needs a multiple viewpoint. In the 'Sadie and Kevin' quintet I shifted my point of view between Sadie and Kevin and I did this in order to give equal weight to each side and not come down in favour of either community. My aim when writing *The Twelvth Day of July*, and its sequels, was to keep a fair balance between the two communities, and not to take sides, so by centering one chapter on the Protestants and one on the Catholics I was able to give them equal weight. If you write a story from more than two or three points of view the reader can be left feeling that he or she has not spent long enough with any of the chatacters and the overall effect might be one of fragmentation. But there are no absolute rules on this and the end result is what matters. An American novelist called Mary McCarthy wrote a very successful novel called *The Group* from the point of view of eight different women.

The next decision to take is that of tense, but I never have any trouble deciding this. I have written all my novels in the past tense though I have used the present for one or two short stories. The present can be very effectively used for short stories as the reader is then make to feel that *this* is happening *now*. Over the length of a novel that can be more difficult to sustain. But it can be useful in a flashback, to mark it out from the main text.

So I pore over my notebook, go for lots of walks, think my way into the characters. Then comes the day to begin! It arrives unbidden. I get up one morning and realise that I *must* start. It is one of the best times in writing as you feel full of excitement and you believe that this will be the best book you've ever written. By the time you've finished you'll have changed your mind, of course, and you'll be feeling critical again. But that, too, is a necessary part of writing since it would be dangerous to become complacent and think that your work is so perfect that it cannot be improved.

The actual beginning, whether it is of a novel or short story or play, is very important. You have to get the attention of the reader immediately so therefore you must come in at a moment of tension or crisis, when something is about to happen. Readers tend to get impatient if they have to wade through a potted history of the characters' families before they get down to the action. My novel *The Guilty Party* opens with the sentence 'It began to look as if the paste might run out.' I want the reader to wonder *what* paste and what are they doing with it? Two girls are putting up posters. It is dark and they are watching for a police car. I try to create a feeling of suspense and to do that you have to be economical. Explanations and descriptions can be worked in later, as unobtrusively as possible. In *Across the Barricades* I subsequently cut out the first eight lines of my original draft and began at the moment when Kevin caught sight of Sadie (see page 60).

And the novel, too, must end at the right moment, after the climax, and not be dragged out. It is a mistake to hold a post mortem, or to explain everything down to the last detail. I believe in leaving endings a little open so that the reader is left with something to think about. At the end of *Across the Barricades* Sadie and Kevin are setting out on the boat to Liverpool to start a new life. So it is an ending and, at the same time, a new beginning. I did go with them on the next stage of their lives in *Into Exile* but I finally leave them in North Wales at the end of *Hostages to Fortune*. I have sometimes been asked what happened to them after that? My answer is: *you* decide.

I work regular hours, from around nine in the morning until five or so in the evening, though for part of that time I might not actually be writing; I might be answering letters, editing, talking on the telephone! I have a study, a very large one, about thirty feet long, with three long windows facing south, and it is full of books, papers, pictures, photographs, all kinds of stuff. Now and then I lose something and have to have a good clear up in order to find it.

I write longhand to begin with, a few pages at a time, as I find it easier to think with a pen in my hand, then I put what I've done on to my word processor and print it out. At the end of the day I will edit it and the following morning start the day by putting the edits on the disc. This makes it easier to get going again. And then I write the next few pages. So in this way, working on small segments at a time, I build up my novel. It takes me about six months to write a novel for young people, and a year to write an adult one.

When I finish the first draft I read it right through at a sitting, making notes, marking parts that need special attention. Sometimes I might put it aside for a week or two so that I will be able to look at it with a more objective eye. And then I begin to work my way through the typescript again, scrutinising everything and rewriting where necessary. I find that the more I have thought out a book beforehand the less rewriting I need to do. I would never sit down in front of a blank page and wonder what to write but I know someone who only knows what the first paragraph will be about when she begins and she writes good novels. There are many different ways to write and it is a matter of finding what suits you personally.

I don't ever wonder what to write about. My subjects seem to find me: they surface from somewhere in my subconscious and drift around in my mind until they begin to gel. I don't write to convey messages, though I have to admit that sometimes there might be one lurking around underneath. I believe that the first aim of a novel should be to entertain, and to stretch the imagination, but I think there is nothing wrong with stretching the mind, too, and making the reader think. The Kevin and Sadie books, as well as telling the story of those two young people, do also carry in them a plea for tolerance and a rejection of prejudice. And in *The Guilty Party* I wanted to make my readers consider the issues of nuclear power, but I had no wish to preach or to brainwash. One of the things I did want to say was: don't be apathetic, think for yourself! The motivation to write this book came from the experiences of my youngest daughter, Jenny, whose involvement with the anti-nuclear movement began at the age of fifteen when she was arrested, like Josie and Emma, for flyposting. She was arrested on several subsequent occasions and finally spent a few days in Holloway Prison. All of this material I used in my novel but Josie is *not* Jenny: she is a figment of my imagination who has many experiences similar to the ones that Jenny had.

A number of themes do seem to recur in my books though I have not been aware of them at the time of writing. One that stands out is that of being displaced—uprooted—for one reason or another, and having to resettle. It is *the* theme of the 'Maggie' quartet. Even the titles reveal that. Sadie and Kevin also suffer displacement, for political and religious reasons, and have to leave their Belfast background and resettle on either side of the Irish Sea, without money, family or friends. In *The Gooseberry*, Ellie faces an upheaval in her life when a prospective stepfather appears on the scene, and in *Strangers in the House* two separate families have to make a new life together when the mother of one family marries the father of the other.

When people are displaced from their pattern of living, they have to re-adjust, to take stock of old values, and assess new ones. Their lives are suddenly wide open, many new things become possible. What will they do, which way will they go? The crossroads of change interest me very much as a writer. Adolescence is in itself a major crossroad in life, a time of great change, and upheaval, which can be both exciting and stressful—for the adolescents themselves but also for the parents!—and I think that this is why I have chosen to write so much about the teenage years.

1

CHAPTER ONE

Sadie Jackson walked along Donegall Place glad to be free of the day's work. The long day behind the shop counter bored her. It was time she was looking for another job. Her mother would blow her head off if she came home saying that. She was always changing jobs. Three in the last year, and each one more tiresome than the last. But she forget about them now for it was a fine spring evening.

She crossed with the crowd over the busy street to the City Hall. As she moved along the wide pavement she heard someone call her name.

"Sadie! Sadie Jackson!"

She looked round. For a moment she could not see who it was that was calling her. The pavement was busy with people heading homewards. Then she saw him. Tall, dark, broader than she had remembered, but with the same bright spark in his eyes. She waited for him to reach her.

"Kevin," she said. "Kevin McCoy."

"It's me all right." He was grinning. "I saw you coming a mile away."

"Haven't seen you for ages. She mused. "Must be near on three years."

"Daresay it is. Funny seeing you again after all this time."

They only lived a few streets away from one another but it might as well have been a few miles. They stood and looked at one another and let the hurrying people push round them.

"Fancy a cup of coffee?" asked Kevin. "Have you time?"

"Don't see why not," said Sadie. There were many good reasons why not, her mother would say, but Sadie was not one to be put off

PUBLICATIONS

Adult novels

Liam's Daughter; The Prevailing Wind; The Tide Comes in; The Headmaster; A Sort of Freedom; The Lord on Our Side; The Second Flowering of Emily Mountjoy; Greenyards; Sisters By Rite; Reasonable Doubts.

Novels for young people

Kevin and Sadie quintet: *The Twelfth Day of July; Across the Barricades; Into Exile; A Proper Place; Hostages to Fortune.*

Maggie quartet: *The Clearance; The Resettling; The Pilgrimage; The Reunion.*

Frying As Usual; The Gooseberry; Snake among the Sunflowers; The File on Fraulein Berg; Strangers in the House; The Winter Visitor; The Freedom Machine; The Guilty Party; Rags and Riches.

A HEAD FOR FIGURES

Joan Lingard

I'm Seb. That's short for Sebastian. But you know that already, from my sister, Sam. Not that you can take every single thing she says for Gospel (as our grandmother would say), but in this case you can.

Granny took to her bed after the fur coat affair. She was sick 'to her stomach'. It was Sunday so the supermarket was closed. By Monday morning, though, she had recovered her appetite sufficiently to demolish a bowlful of porridge, a kipper, two slices of toast and marmalade and five cups of tea. Strong tea. No messing about with any of that herbal stuff our mother drinks, when she's not drinking strong black coffee, that is. She's not consistent, our mother. But you may have gathered that. Granny itemised her breakfast for us when she called in on her way past to work.

'It would do you both good to eat some decent food in the mornings,' she said, rounding on Sam and me, 'instead of yon muck. Uncooked oats and stuff!'

'Muesli's good for them,' said our mother, who was drinking a cup of coffee and not eating at all, which is the usual way she starts the day. She spoke automatically. She was also in her dressing gown, another habit our grandmother disapproves of. She herself washes and dresses as soon as she rises, before a bite is permitted to cross her lips. She has her standards and we are never allowed to forget what they are.

'Look at the two of you!' said Granny. 'No wonder the country is going to the dogs.'

We pulled ourselves up out of our slumps before she could start on about the benefits of a spell in the army. 'They should bring back conscription. It would make men of you.' This can be guaranteed to start a real rave-up of an argument, with Bella, Sam and me ranged on one side. We have anti-nuclear posters pinned up on the shop walls and when Granny is minding the shop she takes them down. She says the government knows what is best for us. She makes us seethe! I didn't feel like an argument that morning. We'd had enough over the fur coat. I finished off my Physics homework.

'You should have had that done last night, son. And you wouldn't be eating and doing your lessons at the same time. I don't know, Isabel! You weren't brought up like that. I always kept you up to the mark.'

Our mother didn't bother to reply. She had other things on her mind. The usual. Money, of course. The electricity bill had come in the morning post, a reminder, the last one, covered with awful warnings in red. Pay up or else.... Our mother had just had time to push it under a bundle of silk scarves lying on the kitchen table before her mother arrived. Granny has her own key so she can walk in unannounced and catch us in various acts.

Sam scraped back her chair and got up, yawning her head off.
'And what time did you get to your bed last night, young lady?'
'Can't remember. Come on and I'll chum you down the road, Gran. I'm ready for off.'

'You're never going to school in *that*?' Granny stared at the garment in which Sam was got up. It was in the 'forties' style, so I had been informed, and it hung rather oddly on Sam, kind of squint-like, and the shoulders made her look like an American football player. (I'd had to duck when *I'd* informed *her* of that.)

Sam put on her innocent look. 'Why not, Gran?'

'I don't know what things are coming to, I'm sure. I mind when children used to go to school looking neat and tidy and wearing uniforms.'

'Well, we don't have to wear uniforms now,' said Sam, picking up a pink satin jacket and slinging it over her shoulders.

'Uniforms leave no room for individuals to express their personalities,' said our mother.

Granny trumpeted.

'Come on,' said Sam and took her arm.

They went off. My mother poured herself another cup of coffee and retrieved the electricity bill from beneath the scarves. She examined it again and sighed.

'I don't know where we're going to get the money from. There's the telephone bill, too, and the amount owing to Mr. McWhitty for the broken window in the shop....'

And no doubt other odd bits and pieces due to this shopkeeper and that.

'How much do we owe altogether, Bella?'

'I've no idea.' She ran her fingers through her hair. It's of the colour that is sometimes described as 'flaming' red and is something Sam and I have inherited from her. An inheritance from her father's side of the family. Carrot tops, Granny calls us and says she can see us coming a mile off, which is not always to our advantage. 'It's all over there,' said my mother.

Over there meant behind the clock that no longer works. It's French ormolu, according to my father, who vows it's worth a fortune, but when he did try to hawk it around the numerous antique shops in the neighbourhood he returned still carrying it and declaring that they didn't know a good thing even when it was shoved under their noses.

I collected the bills and brought them over to the table.

'You count it up, Sebastian. You've got a good head for figures. I'm no use at that kind of thing.'

'You could be if you wanted to. But you don't, do you?'

She was looking at the Articles for Sale in the *Scotsman*. I did a quick count.

'Two hundred and fifty-nine pounds and five pence.'

'Heavens! Where's that going to be found? I've got nine pounds to my name.'

'You could make your customers pay when they buy something.'

'I do! But sometimes they don't have it on them.'

It's not easy having a mother like mine. I tell my friend Hari that but I don't know if he believes me. He thinks she's terribly amusing. He says his own mother is very serious. She's a nurse at the Infirmary. His father's a structural engineer so they both bring home regular salaries and their bills are always paid on time.

'Bella, you've got to learn to be tougher. No money, no deal.'

'I'm sure you'd make a fine business man, Sebastian.'

'Rubbish!' I have plans to be an astronomer. I want nothing to do with selling or with old junk of any kind. 'But if you're going to be in business you'll have to be more business-like.'

'You'll be late for school if you don't hurry.'

I put the bills back behind the clock.

'We'll talk about it later,' I said.

It was three days before I got her back to the topic. Either her friends were in, or Granny.

'You can't just let this ride, Bella,' I said, when I had a chance to get a word in. 'We'll get the electricity cut off, for one thing. And then we'd have to pay to get connected up again.'

'I intend to pay it in the morning. I've borrowed the money from Maudie.'

'*Borrowed.*'

'What else could I do?'

'But you still owe it.'

'I know, Sebastian. What is this—the third degree? Maudie says it'll do at the end of the month. She's all right till then. The only other person I could have gone to is your grandmother and I didn't want to ask her again. Not just yet, at any rate.'

'She's not exactly loaded herself.'

'I'm well aware of that.' My mother's voice was cool now. They're right when they say that money causes a lot of trouble. Lack of it, certainly.

'There is one other avenue we could explore,' she said slowly. 'Your father.'

'Torquil? He doesn't have ten pence to his name.'

'Not according to Maudie. She heard he'd had a big win on the pools. Several hundred.'

'But you don't want to have to ask him for money.'

'No, I don't. You could though, couldn't you?'

'Now listen, Bella!'

'Now listen, Sebastian!'

Why do I always have to be the one who gets the dirty work to do in the family? Sam says that's not true, she does her share. But she never gets sent on missions to Torquil.

'Anyway,' said my mother, 'you ought to visit your father more often.'

I felt like grinding my teeth, only every time I've tried it hasn't come off. I made do with going round to Hari's and sounding off. He lives a street away, in a large, comfortable, *tidy* flat.

'That shop will never pay your bills,' he said, 'even if the customers pay up. Couldn't your mother get a job somewhere?'

'What can you imagine her doing?'

He thought. Clearly, he couldn't see her tending the sick, like his mother. Or delivering the post. She'd meet a friend on the first corner, drop the sack and get into conversation and before long they'd drift off to have a cup of coffee and she'd forget all about the mail.

'I can't believe she is *so* scatty,' said Hari.

'She's a jolly good cook,' I said. And the more exotic the recipes the better. After a couple of lessons on Indian cooking from Hari's mother she could make onion bhajees and chicken biryani better than Mrs. Patel herself.

'She could turn the basement into a restaurant,' suggested Hari.

'Oh no, I don't think that's a very good idea.' I had visions of me doing the waiting and Sam in the kitchen washing up. Our mother would make fantastic dishes and hang about between orders chatting to the customers who would all think she was marvellous and tell Sam and me so.

'I think you will have to talk to your father, you know,' said Hari. 'Especially if he has won money on the football pools.'

I decided to go on Saturday morning. Hari and I arranged to go for a cycle-run down the coast in the afternoon. I would be in need of a good blow of fresh sea air after bearding Torquil in his den.

And some den it is too! He lives in a small flat up a dark smelly stair. The lights always seem to be out and there's usually a stink of tom cat.

I fumbled my way up the three flights and banged on the door. The bell doesn't work. Nothing happened. My eyes were gradually getting used to the gloom. There are two other flats on the landing and the door of one was being opened, just a crack, on its chain. The old man who lives there is afraid of being coshed on the head. He peered out at me.

'Hi!' I said.

'What are you wanting?'

'My father.'

'He'll no be up yet, likely.'

I turned back to my father's door and banged again and rattled the letter box. I squinted inside but saw only more gloom.

'Hey, Torquil!' I yelled into the slit.

And then I heard sounds, Shuffling. Coughing. Yawning. I waited and after a couple of minutes the door finally opened.

'Good morning,' I said.

'Sebastian! It's you, son! Come away in!'

The living room was in a state of chaos. A different kind of chaos from what reigns in our mother's flat. In hers it's colourful and clean; here it was neither.

'Excuse the mess—I've been busy. Start spring cleaning today.'

He yawned. He looked pretty rough. Unshaven, hair on end, eyes like poached eggs. The sight of him annoyed me, yet I felt sorry for him at the same time. I always find it difficult to be with my father.

'I was out with a few friends last night, Seb old man, and we were a shade late getting to our beds, you know how it is. I'll get you some coffee.'

'No, don't bother.'

'Tell you what—we'll go out for breakfast. Hang on a tick till I get my duds on.'

He disappeared and I moved to the window. There wasn't much to see outside, only two women gabbing on the opposite pavement. But on looking over at the window directly across the street, I saw that a woman was watching me. When I looked at her, she drew back behind the edge of her curtain. Hearing a movement behind me, I turned. My father was back. He had shaved and put on a clean shirt and cravat and yellow corduroy trousers.

We went to a café a few minutes walk away. He was known there. He ordered coffee and two bacon rolls and paid in cash which obviously surprised the man behind the counter. So maybe he was in the money after all.

'It's nice of you to come and visit your old pa, Seb.'

Now I was embarrassed and didn't know how I was going to get round to mentioning what I'd come for. The man brought the coffee and bacon rolls and we ate and drank and Torquil called for more coffee and we talked about all sorts of things, like the subjects I was doing at school and his prospects for work.

'I'm in the running for a job at the moment. Think I'm in with a shout, too. Publisher's rep. Well, you know how I love books, Seb. The man and I got on really well. I'm just waiting to hear.'

Eventually, he asked after Bella.

'She's fine.' I braced myself. 'Except that she's short of money.'

'It's the devil of a nuisance, money. Bad business that about the fur coat. Think what we could have done with that lot! A thousand quid!'

'She can't afford to pay the telephone bill.'

'That's why I don't have a phone myself—the bills cripple you.' (He'd had his phone cut off six months before.)

'She needs money, Torquil.' I looked him straight in the eye and kept looking.

'I could let her have a tenner.'

'That wouldn't go very far.' I felt my face getting hot. 'We heard you'd had a win on the pools.'

'Did you now? News travels fast in this damned city.'

'*Did* you win anything?'

'Fifty quid. That's all, honest.' He pulled out his wallet. Inside were two notes, a ten and a one. He held out the ten to me.

'Keep it,' I said and got up.

We parted outside the café.

'Keep in touch, Seb.'

I nodded.

'Tell you what—we'll have an evening out together sometime soon. We could take in a theatre or a film, have a bite to eat afterwards. There's a good Chinese place round the corner. I'll call you, when I get the job.'

Response

OTHER WORLDS

- Why do you think Joan Lingard wrote about such things as Cornish caves when she first started writing as a child? What are your earliest memories of writing, at home and at school?

- In talking about 'Dull deadly old Belfast', what message is Joan Lingard giving to others about the craft of fiction?

- 'Real life is chaotic. Art attempts to bring order to that chaos and give it a form'. Discuss what Joan Lingard means here. Compare her views on autobiography with those of Adèle Geras and Farrukh Dhondy.

- What essential differences does Joan Lingard identify between the short story and the novel, and why does she prefer the latter? What are your views as a reader?

- How does she begin a novel? What lessons are there here for your own creative writing?

- What does she say are the relative merits of writing in the first or third person? How do her views contrast with the other writers in this volume?

- What do we learn from Joan Lingard about the use of different tenses in narrative?

- How important are 'beginnings' and 'endings' to Joan Lingard? What do we learn about her techniques in starting and finishing stories?

- 'There are many different ways to write and it is a matter of finding what suits you personally'. Write a 300 word summary highlighting the process of Joan Lingard's writing.

- Education? Entertainment? Propaganda? How does Joan Lingard see the purpose of her fiction? Discuss in your groups how her views might compare with those of other writers in this volume.

- Why is it that she has chosen to write 'so much about the teenage years'? Do you agree with her views? Think also of other writers who tend to focus on adolescence.

- Look at the draft first page from *Across The Barricades* on page 60, together with the author's comments on page 58. How has the text been amended and to what effect?

A HEAD FOR FIGURES

- How do we know from the opening of this story that it is part of a sequence of stories? Are there any other points in the narrative which refer to what has happened or is going to happen outside 'A Head for Figures'?

- What is the significance of the title of this story?

- What is the relationship between the various characters in the story? Look carefully at how they address one another? What picture do you have of the various households?

- 'Uniforms leave no room for individuals to express their personalities'. How is this statement important to the story as a whole? Do you agree with its message?

- Write short character descriptions of the mother and father.

- Write a couple of further episodes in the lives of Seb and Sam. Then read the novel *Rags and Riches,* and see how close you were to what really happened.

- 'There I am Seb—it doesn't matter that he's male and I'm female'. What do you think? Does the female author write successfully from the male point of view?

- What techniques does Joan Lingard use to reveal a keen sense of place? Compare Berlie Doherty's techniques in 'Gran'.

- Look through the text for examples of Scottish dialect. Make a list of them. Why do you think Joan Lingard included some dialect in the story?

- What are the characteristics of Joan Lingard's style of writing. Look carefully through the text at her use of description, dialogue, vocabulary, length of sentences and paragraphs.

- 'The crossroads of change interest me very much as a writer'. In what ways is this story about change and transition?

- Rewrite 'A Head for Figures' as either a radio or television script. Before you begin, read Berlie Doherty's essay on pages 36–39 and the notes on pages 90–91.

Farrukh Dhondy

A WRITER TALKING

Born 1944, Poona, India. Educated Bishops School, Poona. Degrees from Wadia College, Poona, Pembroke College, Cambridge and Leicester University 1959–1969. Teacher of English, Henry Thornton School, Head of English Department, Archbishop Temples School, Head of Humanities Faculty, Archbishop Michael Ramsey's School. From 1975–1982 published five books, for which he won several awards. 1979 joined the Black Theatre Co-operative, both writing and producing. Experienced in journalism, written for The Guardian, The Listener, Time Out *etc. Writer of multicultural television material both for BBC and Channel 4. From 1984 employed by Channel 4 as Commissioning Editor of Multicultural programmes.*

Dust in the air suspended
Marks the place where a story ended.
T. S. Eliot

The house in which I was brought up, in Poona, India, had very high ceilings made of plaster and wood. The rooms followed one after the other in an uninteresting line, like a tedious argument, and each room was tall, about two to three times the height of an English room—or so I remember it. Each room had, at the top of its east wall, a ventilator, a window or skylight with bars to prevent burglars from getting in, about three feet across and two feet wide.

The high windows had a hinged wooden frame with six square panes of glass and a rope which curled around a pulley and descended into the room. By pulling on the rope one could open or shut the high window and prevent the sparrows from getting in. Open or shut, the windows let in a shaft of light which slanted at different angles into the room, a distinct slab of the sun that got more vertical as the day wore on. In this shaft of light swam a million specks of dust, entering the yellow slant and moving out into the relative darkness of the rest of room.

The dust was always with us, but illuminated only in these shafts of light in that peculiar house through those particular windows. The sun, everywhere almost always in an Indian day, didn't elsewhere strip naked the air that I breathed.

Those dancing shafts of dust, the eternal motion to which they seemed dedicated, the fact that a torch wouldn't pick them out, only the light from the tall windows, played in my imagination and came back to me several times. When studying physics we were told about small particles. We learnt about Brownian motion. I had to do the maths related to these particles and motions, but in my mind's eye, the world of jiving dust made the idea visible. So also when I read about corpuscles and sperm, the picture returned—of specks dancing in the sunlight. God too I was told was everywhere but invisible: like the dust made visible in slices, I thought.

Years later I read the Eliot poem with which I've started this essay. I was in England at a university and it was my first Christmas vacation. My English friends, and the rest of them of course, had gone back home to spend the vacations with their families. The college in Cambridge emptied out. I was asked by the Head Porter to move into rooms and found myself an attic in a street close by. My money had to feed me and the gas meter, so I spent the days towards Christmas in bed under the blankets, and the rest of the time I went to the centrally heated library and picked books, sometimes novels, sometimes short stories, sometimes poems (I was studying physics) and read them, daring myself to finish a book before I bought myself a meal.

The library had high windows. 'Dust in the air suspended marks the place . . .' I read, and remembered the windows of my childhood home. There was only the grey light of a woolly English winter through the windows and the conical beams of yellow from the reading-lamp shades. Not a speck of dust. Reality had gone underground, had willed itself invisible. There was no visible dust in the air suspended. I didn't know any English stories. The library, the three others who shared, with polite coughs and apologetic shuffling, the room with me for the whole day, held no memory or incident on which I could remark.

In my house in Poona, in the evenings, after dark, they said ghosts came to the barred windows, the low ones, and hovered on the veranda with lamps. The place had associations for me. The dust marked a spot where several stories ended.

Everything I've said above is true and not true. None of it is strictly true. There were shafts of light, sure, there were the windows. I don't know when I first heard of Brownian motion, or first read the poem I've quoted. I don't know that I thought about anything when I read the poem, I was probably carrying the book about to be flash, to show anyone who was looking that I read English poetry.

I didn't spend my entire first holiday in England in rooms. I had invitations to the homes of several friends and accepted one or two of them. But if you don't tell lies you can't tell stories.

There is a point to telling this story. The point is that the material of one's stories is all around one, but it's invisible. Maybe its hidden in the air, like specks of dust which you're breathing all the time, but to see them, to watch them move, to associate them with other things, theories, sciences, discoveries, one's own and those that belong to everyone, you need a column of sunlight.

One of the writers I admire the most, V. S. Naipaul, [infuriating though his opinions are] wrote a book called *The Enigma Of Arrival*. It is partly a novel and partly an autobiographical piece in which he tells how he came from Trinidad to Britain to study, how he always wanted to be a writer, and how it took a particular illumination for him to understand what the material of his writing was going to be.

Another writer, philosopher and historian, C. L. R. James, who is a friend, says to me (at the time of writing this he is 87 years old) that he started writing before he was ten. His first story was an imitation of *The Last Of The Mohicans*. He turned the setting to Trinidad and presented it to his first readership—his mother—who promptly identified the source from which he had cribbed it and encouraged him to try something of his own. It was probably years before C.L.R. produced a story that was uniquely Trinidadian and his own.

It's the most difficult matter this, the discovery of what one is to write. The only certain thing about it is that it's right under your nose but until you see it, you don't.

I don't mean to imply that one writer is doomed to one chunk of subject matter for ever. His or her life changes, and the matter changes with it. The very 'professional' writers, using that term for those who earn their living by it, are asked in our world to write things to order. This is probably more true of the TV writer, who may be asked to contribute an episode to *The Bill* or to originate another *Brookside* or *EastEnders*, with a given set of rules and even perhaps a given set of characters. Writers who come later to the game of a TV series or a soap are given a typed or printed list of rules and characteristics to which they should adhere. No shame in it, cutting coats according to cloth, it's still tailoring! Your imagination hasn't woven the fabric, but you still have to know how to stitch.

Let me confess: I used to be a school teacher. Teaching English. I now work as a writer and as a commissioning editor for TV, which means that I assess other people's scripts and ask some writers to write this or that and refuse other writers the chance to have their scripts made into TV plays or films. Having done this for some years I realise the folly of my ways as a teacher.

As other English teachers no doubt do, I would walk into a class and ask the thirty or so young people gathered there to 'write a story' based on a theme or an outline or an idea which I would supply. If I said 'write anything you like' most of them would write gibberish. Full marks for following instructions. I had said 'anything you like.' It was better to set the essay or the story.

To write such a story, supplied in outline by someone else, may be a useful exercise in order to assess sentence structure, spelling, logic, the ability to think out a plot etc. but it won't produce exceptional pieces of narrative. There is no course in schools which assists pupils to find their material. Or is there? The professional writer finds it hard enough to use characters and outlines created by script editors, producers and other writers; and he or she has usually come to the practice through presenting some original work.

I need to start again. I've said I spent my boyhood in India, in Poona, which was four hours from Bombay by train. My uncle, who worked in Bombay and came home to Poona once every month at weekends, brought with him, on the train, paperbacks which he had picked up from the pavement stalls. One of these was a volume called *The Short Stories of O'Henry*. It fell into my possession, the corners of the pages black where my uncle had used the edges to clean his nails. For the first time I read stories whose ends I had not anticipated. In later years I found out that this quality of turning events round with the last paragraph is called 'sting-in-the-tail', but before that the scorpion had infected me. Nowadays O'Henry is not considered a great writer, and he is rarely taught in British schools.

Admiration, the desire to imitate, is perhaps the first step to wanting to write. I don't think I ever thought I could write like O'Henry, but I am now sure that reading those stories made me want to write them. My uncle spent years coming home from Bombay, less and less frequently as he settled into his life in the big city. As a result I read books which I would not have otherwise.

He gave me two books, paperbacks by someone called Albert Camus, *The Fall* and *The Outsider*. Later he brought me Lawrence Durrell's *Alexandria Quartet*. The first two taught me that writing stories was a rum business, all to do with death and sex and things more dangerous, more risky, more challenging than the heroics that I and my friends admired—cricket, hockey, the imitation of Elvis Presley. And the *Alexandria Quartet* told me that writing was about showing off, the words you knew that no-one else knew, the seedy places that you had been, the odd and mysterious and dangerous people one could encounter if one was a writer.

None of the plans I had for writing worked out. I wrote fragments of novels like Camus and like Durrell and I couldn't read them back to myself without getting bored.

The next time I wrote seriously was for the newspapers in India. I was angry at being thrown out of rooms in Cambridge for what I thought were racist reasons. I compared notes with my Indian and black friends. I wrote an article which *The Times Of India* newspaper accepted. It started my career in occasional political journalism.

I came to London when I'd finished at Cambridge and I worked at odd jobs and joined a radical group of black power people. I won't explain what that meant in those days, but it was dedicated work and involved me writing several articles a week for a paper that was hand-printed and distributed by members of the group.

I began to teach to earn a living (not out of a sense of mission, I never did subscribe to the theory that the people I was teaching needed me or my message in any way). I enjoyed it immensely. I continued to write the political stuff, pretty severe pieces about school, about black people I knew or had worked with, all in the shape of real/fictional articles. I didn't know how a respectable member of the publishing profession read any of it, but one day, like a proverbial good fairy asking you for a wish, came this letter asking to meet me in order to discuss the writing of some fiction. Mr. Editor, who perhaps prefers to remain anonymous, asked me for a book. I agreed to write it and did.

It didn't take me long to think that my subject would be. He wanted a book of stories about Asian teenagers and I knew some as pupils, some as friends, some as children of friends, and knew myself as an Asian teenager, and the rest I asked about or made up. No, that's a lie. All writing starts in observation. Someone said the film *ET* is about a boy and his dog. What they mean is that this is the observed phenomenon, the love between a boy and a non-human. The rest is invention. Plots can be, writing can't. There was another book after that first one, and then some stories and then *Come To Mecca* which I wrote as an entry to a short story competition.

The competition asked for stories about multicultural Britain. That could mean a lot of things. Perhaps to those who set the competition it was a way of searching for material for a market. For me it was different, I worked in a school with blacks and whites and lots of trouble and I *was* multicultural Britain. But I didn't want to write about myself because the very words told me that the publishers had an audience in mind. It so happened that I had the same audience in mind because five days a week I used to teach a mixed class in every sense; sex, race, a narrow range of social class, but still a range.

One thing a short story must do is condense time. A novel can take its time. James Joyce wrote a book about eighteen hours which took me eighteen weeks to read. A short story is more of a chess game. With a time limit.

If you read the story that accompanies this essay (*Free Dinners*) you will notice that several years pass in its telling. The narrator starts in the first year of his secondary school and goes through to the time when he is an apprentice, a time span of maybe nine or ten years.

I didn't spend ten years observing this one couple. I watched one couple in the first year and at the same time another in the fifth year and just after that a third who had left school.

I've said that all stories start in observation, but the terrors they capture are not purely observed, they may be felt. I'll say something I haven't thought before. The girl in the story *Free Dinners* becomes someone who inspires pity, wonder, maybe admiration for an inner strength. It never started from ideology in my head. I don't think short stories can be written that way. If you have good anti-racist intentions or good 'ist' intentions of any sort, join the appropriate boy scout or girl guide troupe. Do good works. Don't insult the craft of fiction by reducing it to any form of propaganda.

In writing it, I didn't think out or plot the precise conclusion of the story. It worked itself that way, and if there is an explanation for it in my experience, it is further back and more painful than the make-believe projection of one of my ex-pupils as a prostitute.

Neither could the story be in my own voice. It had to be told in the voice of Tony because it is about him growing up through observation as much as it is about the girl.

As always with short stories I drafted and redrafted it on my typewriter. I always feel my wrist tiring if I write longhand and sometimes I can't read my own writing. I let this particular story lie about for a few months before I finally reworked it.

Some years after it was first published, the BBC asked me to rewrite several of my stories as TV plays. I chose six of them and considered writing up *Free Dinners* as one. I told myself that it couldn't be done for technical reasons. There was too much of Tony's voice in it. The TV audience would perhaps not accept a young man talking at them from behind the screen. That was the way I thought of introducing Tony's voice, as 'voice over' before and sometimes during the dramatised scenes.

In the end I rejected the idea of dramatising that particular story, not for technical reasons—I think I could have solved that difficulty—but because there is something about the story which I would never be able to convey by making it totally objective, out there on the screen. That something, I think, is a real deep-down memory of terror that went into the writing.

In my school in Poona there were very street-wise boys from Bombay, the big and corrupt city. They brought with them to the dormitories (it was partly a boarding school) stories of the viciousness of Bombay. In particular I remember listening with a creeping sense of shame, on behalf of I don't know whom, the first description of the trade of prostitution. I was nine years old and was just coming to terms with a garbled understanding of the bare but confusing facts of sex between human beings. In a darkened dormitory some kid told the story of any woman alighting at Bombay's great terminus railway station being kidnapped and recruited into slavery. The wretched child, obsessed by this fact, had some photographs from a magazine to prove his point, women behind bars in the prostitute district of Bombay, strangely made blind by the plaster of anonymity that newspaper editors use over the eyes of the subjects of risky photographs. I had bad dreams. I prayed that none of my female relatives would ever go to Bombay. By the time I came to write the story of Lorraine, the memory of these bad dreams was dim, the horror had long past. For me. But maybe not for Tony.

PUBLICATIONS

Novels

East End at Your Feet, Macmillan, 1976. Won the *Other Award.*
The Siege of Babylon, Macmillan, 1977.
Come to Mecca, Collins, 1978. Won the *Other Award* and the Collins/Fontana *Award for Books about Multicultural Britain.*
Poona Company, Gollancz, 1980.
Trip Trap, Gollancz, 1982.

Stage plays

Mama Dragon (1980).
Trojans (1982).
Vigilantes (1984).
Film Film Film (1985).

TV drama

BBC Series of six plays featuring *Come To Mecca,* 1982.
No Problem series I, II, II (co-written with Mustapha Matura), 1983/84/85.
Tandoori Nights, Channel 4, 1984.
The Empress And The Munshi, Central TV, 1984.
King Of The Ghetto, BBC, 1986.

FREE DINNERS

Farrukh Dhondy

Lorraine was in my first-year class at school and the only reason I noticed her was because she was on free dinners like me. We was the only two in that class who had to take the shame of it. We had a right nasty teacher, Mr. Cobb, (so you know what we used to call him). Just the way he called your name at the end of the register made you crawl and feel two feet small. He'd collect the money from the other kids and make Lorraine and me queue up separately at his table. Not that he ever said anything to us. He just finished with the regular kids and then announced 'Free Dinners' even though there was only two of us.

After the first week of that, I couldn't take it no more, so I used to go and sit in the bogs when the dinner register was taken and go down to the office after and get my mark. That was dangerous too, 'cos when some wally set fire to the bogs, I got the blame. The register never seemed to bother Lorraine. She would stand up in front of me, and even at that age she looked unconcerned with the way the world treated her. She had a look of thinking about something else all the time, and had tight little lips which showed you that she was right tough and determined—and she was skinny as barbed wire.

She was a coloured kid, or at least she was a half-caste or something like that. We always called them 'coloured' when I first went to school because we didn't think there was nothing wrong with it; but after, some of them would thump you if you called them 'coloured'. They didn't like that, they wanted to be called 'black'. I'm not really sure to this day what she was, on account of never seeing her mum or dad. All the other kids would talk about their mums and dads and the gear they had indoors, but Lorraine always kept herself to herself. She wasn't much to look at and she didn't get on with any of the other girls, because some of the white girls were right snobbish. The other coloured kids would talk black when the teachers weren't there, and they left Lorraine out because she never.

She was good at sports and she was good at drama. I wouldn't have noticed her, I tell you, because at that age I wasn't interested in girls. The other lads would talk about what they done with girls and that, but I couldn't be bothered, and because I was skint till the fourth year, I never took no girls out or even let the kids in the class know who I fancied. It was a girl in our class called Wendy. She had a nasty tongue, but I liked her. I remember the first time Lorraine and I stood in the free dinner queue, Wendy said, 'She looks like she needs them and all.' The other kids laughed, and I must have blushed all over my fat cheeks. Old Cobblers didn't tell Wendy off or have a go at her, and Lorraine just pretended she didn't hear.

I kind of hated Lorraine. I knew that the rest of the class thought that we was tramps. I knew it wasn't her fault, but she was kind of showing me up just by her existence. She wouldn't go and hide in the girls' bogs, she'd just stand there in front of Cobblers' desk and be the only one in the class on free dinners, and because she was there the other kids would know I was hiding, because Cobblers would say, 'Biggs has gone underground again,' or something.

When Lorraine started coming flash the other kids began to take notice of her. In our fifth year she was going to get the drama prize. She was good at acting, and the drama teacher had sent her to some competition which she'd won. She dressed her up as a page boy and gave her a boy's part from Shakespeare. It made her look nice, because she had short hair and sort of squarey shoulders, even though she was as thin as a broomstick. I was the captain of the football team and had to pick up the cup for the team on prize day. The deputy head called all the kids who'd won prizes into the hall and told us that the Bishop would be there to give us our prizes that evening and how we should make sure that our parents came. She went on and on about school uniform and what the boys should wear and how we should wash our hair and have clean hands for the Bishop to shake. Then she turned to the girls and did a right turn, showing them how to curtsy, which made them giggle. Then she goes, 'I've told you this before, but I'll rehearse it with you again. You won't be allowed to accept any prize unless you're decently dressed, and that means school uniform. If you don't have one, you'll have to get a skirt below the knee, a clean white blouse and blue cardigan. And no blue and green tights. I want all the girls to wear flesh-coloured tights.'

'Whose flesh, miss?' Lorraine asked.

The deputy head stopped as though Lorraine had clocked her one. Some of the girls giggled.

'Go and wait outside the hall for me, will you, Lorraine?' she said quietly, and Lorraine walked out, saying, 'I only asked a simple question,' and she knew that at least a few admiring eyes were following her.

It was the first time I had heard Lorraine say anything coloured, anything to show that she knew she was coloured. I'll tell you straight up, that if anyone else had said that, I would have thought it was too flash. The coloured kids in our year were a load of wallies. They didn't want to mix with the rest of us. When they had a laugh it was on their own, and they collected together in the fifth-year room at lunch times and after school and took over the record player and just played their dub and reggae and that. Some of them were all right, but some of them just liked to come flash with you.

When we gathered that evening in room B12, behind the stage, waiting to get the prizes, Lorraine walked in looking a real state. She had on black velvet hot-pants and a black silk shirt and had made herself up to look right tarty with crimson lipstick and heavy eyeshadow. The girls sort of turned away when she came in and the boys started making remarks and whistling to take the piss and I was looking, just staring at her because she didn't half look different, dressed like that. Then the deputy came in and threw a fit. Her jaw dropped down to her tits. She rushed Lorraine out of the room and we all ran to the door to hear them arguing in the corridor.

The deputy was telling her that she could still get her prize if she'd wash her face and change in a spare skirt and blouse that she'd give her. But Lorraine wasn't having it. It was as if she'd turned beastly at sunset or something. She gave the deputy some nasty cheek and the deputy didn't turn the other one, she just tried to tell her to 'clear off the premises', and Lorraine said she'd wear what she liked out of school time because it was her culture, and the deputy said she was still in school time if she was inside the gates. When the deputy came back in our room, she was sort of blinking to hold back her tears, looking like Lorraine had really told her which stop to get off at. Lorraine didn't collect the prize of course.

It was after that prize day that Lorraine became a bit of a loud mouth. I heard her telling some of the coloured kids that the deputy head was jealous of her and prejudiced, and didn't want her to be an actress, and wanted to shove her off to work in a laundry. And Lorraine took her revenge.

We were in the maths class and the deputy came in and put her coffee mug, which she always carried around the corridors of the school, down on the teacher's desk. She asked the teacher's permission and began telling us about some fight on a bus in which our kids had duffed up the conductor or something. Everyone was listening quietly and Lorraine, pretending to talk to another girl, said, 'I bet she'll blame the blacks.' The deputy didn't pay any attention, just finished what she was saying and then asked the maths teacher if she could have a word with him outside. She was a bit put out, so she left her coffee on the desk and went out with him.

When they stepped out, Lorraine got up from her desk and went to the front of the class and looked in the coffee cup. We thought she'd take a drink and some kids said, 'Go on, dare you.' So Lorraine turns to the class and says,

'What, drink *her* coffee, and get rabies?' and she cleared her throat with a loud hawking sound and gobbed into the cup, a huge slimy gob. She stirred it with her pencil and without a smile to the rest of the class, sat down again. The two teachers came back in the room and the deputy took her coffee and split. The maths geezer said that Lorraine was to report to the Head's office at 12.30. Lorraine said, 'Yes, sir,' and the maths feller said, 'You ought to be given a taste of your own rudeness.' The kids all laughed and he didn't know why.

It was at that time I think that I began to admire Lorraine. I told myself that if I got the chance I'd ask her out, but I didn't want any of the lads to know what was on my mind because, for one, they didn't ever take black girls out, not the mob I moved with in school and, for another, they thought Lorraine was some kind of looney loner. That's why I didn't ask her to the fifth-year dance, and good job I didn't, because she came to the dance with a group of black boys from Brixton and they pushed past the teachers at the door and began to act like they owned the place. I think Lorraine just brought them to show that she moved with the dread locks or whatever they liked to call themselves. It wasn't going to be a particularly good party with no booze or nothing.

These kids brought their own records and they broke up the dance when they started threatening the guy who was playing DJ for the evening. The guy stopped the music and the teachers switched all the bright lights on and suddenly the place was full of teachers and schoolkeepers, and when Lorraine's crowd started arguing back, they called the police. A lot of the white kids began to drift off, because a blind man could see there was going to be trouble.

I was watching Lorraine. She looked as thought she knew she had gone too far. She was trying to cool it and reason with her black friends, but they shoved her aside and shaped up like they were going to duff up the DJ. Then someone said the police had arrived outside and the black kids legged it. Lorraine got into a lot of trouble on account of that scene. Some of the kids, the next day, the white kids, were talking as though they were scared of Lorraine. The blacks were laughing about it. Lorraine wasn't laughing with them; she was just pretending she hadn't been there and getting on with her classwork. That's what I liked about her. She created hell and behaved as though she was the angel of the morning.

At this time I was going out with Wendy. She was right hard, harder than a gob-stopper, and she always settled arguments with her fists. I suppose I was a bit fed up of her really. She never let me touch her all the time we was going out. She was a bit of a tom-boy and didn't even want to be kissed. Her dad was a copper and strict. I had to take Wendy home at eleven even if we went to a party. I was fair sick of her, even though she was a good-looker, nice face, big tits and always dressed flash.

I wanted to ask Lorraine out and I knew that Wendy would do her nut if she found out. I brought up the subject once with the lads I used to circulate with, and they figured that Lorraine was right easy, that she'd let you do anything with her. They said the black guys from Brixton who she went out with wouldn't hang around her for nothing. They figured she wouldn't go out with a white bloke. I didn't say nothing to them, but one day after school when I knew she had drama club. I waited around in the year-room and played records till the other kids had gone home and started chatting her up.

I was quite surprised when she said she'd go to the pictures with me. We fixed it for the next time she was staying late at school. I didn't tell the lads in school about our date, but I phoned my friend Tony, who lived in his own flat and told him that I might drop in for a bit after the pictures if my bird fancied staying out. I had six quid on me that day. I met Lorraine up the Elephant in the evening and I said I wanted to go to the Swedish movies, they were really good, but she laughed at me and took me to some crummy film about some stripper girl in Germany or some place.

Lorraine didn't talk silly like Wendy. She had sort of two sides to her. She was a bit posh and she was also hard black. She'd go to the pictures that snobs would see, and she'd want to go to plays and things, and then she'd also talk rude and swear in Jamaican and that.

Until I took her out, I never knew she talked so much. She was explaining the film to me. It was nice listening to her. She wasn't thick like Wendy. When she started explaining why the stripper done what she done, it was nice. It was like I'd had six pints and all the words made sense to me, or like I didn't care if they made sense or not, there was something new and exciting about them.

Then after the pictures I asked her if she fancied going down to my friend's place, because he might be having a party and she gave me a smile and said she was hungry.

'Fancy some chips?' I asked.

'I'm going to take you out to a meal, Pater,' she said. That touched me. It fair knocked me out, to tell you the truth. We went to this Chinese joint she knew in the West End. She was putting on the style, but I didn't mind.

When we sat down they brought this tea that smelt like bad after-shave. She started pouring it out and knocking it back and I said I couldn't drink tea without milk and three teaspoons of sugar and she laughed.

'What do you want to eat, Pete?' she asked. 'Don't worry, I'll pay.'

'I'll have a plaice and chips,' I said, not looking at the menu.

'Don't be so thick, "darling",' she said, pronouncing the 'darling' like one of the girls in the film we'd just seen.

'Steak and chips, then,' I said.

'You can stop playing Cockney hero now,' she said.

'I ain't eating no ying yang food,' I said.

She just grabbed the menu from my hand and went into splits. She split herself, and on my mother's life I could not see the joke, so I said I wasn't hungry, but to tell you the truth my stomach was growling like a waterfall.

I sat and watched as she swallowed all the spaghetti and stuff. She kept saying I ought to try some, but I wasn't going to show myself up. If I'd said one thing, then I was going to stick to it. 'I'm not hungry,' I said.

When I left her at the bus-stop she asked me if I'd enjoyed my dinner. Real flippin' cheeky she was.

'Best portion of plaice and chips I've had in years, really crisp,' I said, just to show I didn't have any hard feelings, even though my feelings were harder than exams. I'd paid for the dinner. I'd insisted.

'I've always enjoyed free dinners,' she said, as she got on the 133 to Brixton from the Elephant. That's the kind of brass you don't need to polish, I thought, as I walked back home with my hands in my pockets.

I rang up Tony and told him it didn't work out. I tried to take Wendy out again, but she was going with this geezer from Scotland Yard who had a blue Cortina and she told me she didn't want to go out with schoolboys. I'd have asked Lorraine out again, but I felt she was only tolerating me and she didn't fancy me one bit. I thought about her a lot. She was a funny girl. I didn't speak to her in school after that evening. I don't know what it was, I can't quite put my finger on it, but I felt she was telling me somehow to keep my distance. When I was going with Wendy, I always got the feeling that she'd do her nut if I packed her in, but with Lorraine it was like she expected nothing, wanted nothing, she'd take what came, and wait for more to come.

Then she started taking the mick. It was in a General Studies class in the sixth form, and this teacher was going on about why the Irish were thick or something. He was saying that everybody thought that everybody else was thick, that it was natural, and if the British thought the Irish were not so smart, then the Jews thought the British were not so smart and the Americans thought that the British were all snobs or all Cockneys talked in rhyming slang and the like. Then Lorraine started shooting her mouth. There was only twelve of us in that class and we sat around a table in the sixth-form suite and this geezer never stopped talking about politics and racial relations and prejudice and all that crap. Lorraine always talked to him like she was the only one in the class and we was out in the playground playing marbles and she was on telly.

'That's what all white people think,' she said, 'It's just stupidness. They think Pakis are all Oxfam and niggers live in trees, and Chinese food is ying yang food.'

I knew she was getting at me. Then the geezer asked us for our views, so I said, 'I reckon that a lot of it is true, that blacks do live off Social Security, because there's a black feller on our estate and he drives a Benz, and polishes it up every Saturday and when you see him he's always got a new suit and he goes with white slags, a new one every two hours, and he never works. It's nothing to do with prejudice, it's just that a lot of white people pay a lot of tax and rates and that the blacks come in and take Social Security . . .'

'And eat a lot of free dinners,' Lorraine said.

She was a bitch. She never talked to me after that. Not till we left school.

I'd meet someone from school down the Walworth Road and they'd say, 'Watcha, Pete,' and we'd have a talk. I wanted to be an architect, but I had to get my City and Guilds Draughtsman's exams first, so I was working with this firm on an apprenticeship. We'd talk about this and that and how much lolly we was taking home and about the old teachers and the old times. All the white kids I met from school knew that Wendy had gone for an Old Bill, and she was saying 'hello, hello, hello' instead of 'watcha'. We didn't talk about the black kids, except for Keith, who wasn't like the rest of them and was trying to be a draughtsman himself. If I saw any of the blacks I'd been in school with, they would raise their hands, or just blank me, and we'd pass without a word. I thought a bit about Lorraine. If I met her again, I told myself, I'd ask her out, show her that I'd learnt a thing or two, I'd planned it all out in my head. We'd go to the same cinema and see some posh movie or other, whatever was running, and then I'd take her to a Chinese and order a Won-ton Soup and Crab in Ginger, Char Si Pong, the lot, just to show her that old Pete had learnt a thing or two with the lads at the firm who were fond of a curry or of a Chinese or pizza after a hard Friday night's drinking down the local. The lads would talk about a Vindaloo and a Madras as though they was bloody veterans of the Burmese campaign.

When I actually met her, there was no chance. Well, I didn't exactly meet her. I just saw her and we exchanged a few words. It was like this. I was round Kilburn way, 'cos our office has a branch up there, and I was told to go and discuss some designs with a top geezer in our firm who worked in Kilburn. The lads from the Kilburn office sussed me out and, after, we went for a drink in a pub round their way. I didn't know them much, but I strung along.

The pub was a young scene, Friday night boppers from round the top end of the Edgware Road. There were lights popping all over the ceiling and huge mirrors on the walls which were otherwise plastered with old newspapers to give the place the look of being in the know. Up the end of the bar was this geezer doing the disco, leaning over his tube microphone and running down the soul.

'We're gonna have some dancing in a piece, Pete,' Sol told me. 'This is a nice scene, topless go-go, strippers, a pint of real ale, a real good time.'

So the spotlight came on the stage and the disco geezer introduced the dancer. We were at the bar. A few of the lads had grabbed stools and I was standing with my pint with my back to the stage and the dance floor. When the music stopped I looked around. You could have knocked me down with a feather. Just outside the circle of the spotlight, like a ghost, like a bloody shivering ghost, stood Lorraine, in a dressing-gown which she was urging off her shoulders. Some black guy was waiting at the corner of the stage to catch it as it dropped. As the DJ finished his introduction, she strolled into the light in heels and gold knickers with purple tassles dangling from them and no bra. The pub had turned its attention to her, though I could see that the fellers in my mob were pretending to take it cool. They were all screwing her and giving off that they weren't interested at all.

The strobe came on and the green and blue lights began flashing. Lorraine with her haunted face and wiry body began her dance, her skinny pair of legs like those of a delicate race-horse, slim, with the muscles running on the bone, shifting with some hesitance.

'I heard it through the grapevine, no longer will you be mine,' sang Marvin Gaye, and the mob I was with began to hoot and slap.

'Look at the state of it,' said Sol. 'Blimey, I'd rather go to Madame Tussaud's and see the Chamber of Horrors.'

In the dark she couldn't see us, she couldn't have known where the voices were coming from. Between the stage and us there were these pillars, and I felt like disappearing behind one of them. She was dancing good, mind you, but it was true that she didn't have much meat on her.

She was a mover, give her that. And she had some guts getting up in front of that mob and doing her thing.

'Oxfam,' one of the lads shouted, and the faces in the darkness tittered.

'Spare ribs,' Sol shouted, and she danced on.

'Knock it off,' I said. 'Don't show us up.'

'Spare ribs,' someone else shouted from the far end of the pub. She had small breasts, flat on her sinewy body. Of course she heard the voices, heard the laughter, but her expression didn't change. She was dancing for all she was worth, and her body moved gracefully through the tune, but there was no sex in it, if you know what I mean. She wasn't no topless dancer, and if she didn't realize it, the governor of the pub should've.

'Spare ribs.' They'd picked it up at the other end of the pub and were trying to give her the slow hand-clap. They were going at it like it was the first laugh they'd had that week.

The record finished and Lorraine stepped hastily out of the spotlight. The DJ quickly flipped turntables and started some soul sounds. I watched her as her man gave her the dressing-gown and she rushed into the ladies.

'The gaffer's not going to have her again,' the barman said.

I left my pint on the bar and waited till she came out of the ladies. She was wearing a trouser suit and a band around her forehead. As I approached her I could see her mascara was smudged and she looked like she'd rather be on the Flying Scotsman to hell than right there in that pub. She was in a hurry, but she saw me and recognized me.

'Hello, Lorraine,' I said, not knowing what else to say. I felt the lads had treated her something rotten, something shameful, and on my life if I'd been able to, I would have got them publicly on their knees to her.

She was as surprised as I was.

'I didn't know you hung around my ex-beat,' she said.

'I didn't know you'd started professional dancing,' I said.

'Well, you heard what the customers thought,' she said.

I wanted to ask her for a drink, but it was the wrong place, the wrong moment. I wanted to tell her that I'd often thought of her, that now more than ever I wondered where she'd got to, what she was doing, how she kept herself. Her man come up and touched her elbow.

'I'll see you, Pete,' she said.

'Yeah,' I said.

'I'm dancing in another pub,' she said. 'Half an hour. Rough stuff, this, earning your dinners,' and she smiled and walked away. I went back to my pint.

The last time I saw her was very brief. I met her on the pavement in Soho. It was raining. I'd finished my time at the firm and I'd bought this car and dropped my mate and girl-friend off at Gerrard Street. I'd gone to park the car. I saw her coming from a few yards down. She was with an old bald geezer in a posh raincoat. She was hanging on to his arm, dressed to the hilt, made up like a wedding cake. She looked stoned, too, unsteady on her feet.

'I saw you first this time,' she said.

She stopped in front of me and smiled, and her mouth opened but her eyes stayed distant, like I'd known them, like they were when she was thinking of other things when we'd been there, children in the first year of school. The old man stood a little way behind her and she behaved as though he wasn't there. She put her fingers on my tie, and said, 'How are you, Peter?'

I stepped back a bit.

'I'm just going to see some friends,' I said.

'Have you seen anyone from the old school?' she asked. 'I haven't seen any of them bastards,' she added, veering on her feet.

'No, no, I haven't,' I said.

'Oh, hang on,' she said. 'I saw your girl-friend Wendy. You know what she said to me?'

'Yes, Wendy,' I said. 'She's in the police, isn't she?'

'She too damn feisty. She catch me on my business,' Lorraine said, her accent suddenly becoming black.

'Oh, oh,' I said. 'You been nicking from Woolworth's again, Lorraine?'

I shuffled my feet. I could see it coming.

'You see this, Pete,' Lorraine said, taking one step back and pointing with a flowing hand at the pavement. 'This here is the street. Your Wendy don't want me to walk the street and she is a po-lis.' She nodded. Now I could see that she was drunk, but her eyes which stared into mine looked sober as the rising sun. 'She don't like me walk the street, our Wendy,' she said.

'Yes,' I said. 'What do you expect from the Old Bill? She wasn't ever my girl, Lorraine!'

'You want to get out of the rain, Pete,' she said. She began to walk past me dragging the old geezer after her.

'Pete,' she said, and turned round as though she'd forgotten something. 'Pete, I'll see yuh.' She was facing me again and she turned to the old geezer who looked impatient to shove off. 'It's Pete, my old school mate. Pete, this is Mr. Smith who's just going to buy me a free dinner.'

Response

A WRITER TALKING

- The first few pages of this essay illustrate two points about writing:
  'If you don't tell lies you can't tell stories.'
  'The material of one's stories is all around one, but it's invisible . . . to see them you need a column of sunlight'.
  Explain in your own words what is meant by these two points.
  Why do you think Dhondy begins with the quotation from T. S. Eliot?
  What is added to your understanding of these comments by the story Dhondy tells about the windows in his house in Poona?

- Looking back on his own time as a teacher, what does the author say that he did wrong when asking pupils to write English essays? Talk about your own experience of 'writing for an audience'.

- Why is it that stories with a 'sting-in-the-tail' capture the imagination, as they obviously did for Farrukh Dhondy? Make a list of stories that you have read which have a surprise ending. Which are your favourites and why? Discuss them in your groups.

- What lessons about writing did the author gather from his reading of Albert Camus and Lawrence Durrell? Look up some examples of their work.

- 'All writing starts in observation . . . The rest is invention. Plots can be, writing can't'. What do you understand by these words?

- To what extent would you describe 'Free Dinners' as an autobiographical story? Think carefully about what the author writes on pages 68–72.

- Farrukh Dhondy asserts that fiction should not be 'propaganda'. What are your views on this? Look up the meaning of 'propaganda'. If a writer feels strongly about something or has experiences that s/he wishes to share, at what point does entertainment end and education begin? Discuss this subject in your groups, with reference to any of the writers in this volume.

FREE DINNERS

- How would you describe the style and tone of Dhondy's writing? List some examples of his language usage to support your views.

- Write a short character description of Pete, including what it is which attracts him to Lorraine.

- What do we learn in the story about (a) the writer's views on multi-cultural schools, and (b) the attitudes of the pupils towards living in a mixed society?

- Thinking about what all the writers in this collection say about narrative viewpoint—see pages 68–69 in particular for Dhondy's comments—what does this story gain and perhaps lose from being written in the first-person? Imagine the story written in a third-person narrative. What difference would it make?

- Farrukh Dhondy says on page 71 that he finally rejected the idea of turning 'Free Dinners' into a television script. You take up the BBC offer! Re-write the story as either a radio or television script, bearing in mind the advice offered on pages 90–91.

- Thinking about the author's views on the subject, would you describe 'Free Dinners' as a story with a message? Is it ever a tale of propaganda?

- In both his essay and his story, the author plays with time. How does he manipulate the passing of time in 'Free Dinners'? Do you think he is successful in organising the narrative in the way that he does?

- What is the significance of the title of the story? Think of some alternative titles which would highlight the author's themes and ideas.

- Re-read the story and draw up the following chart to fill in as you read.
  Be selective—don't take every event but choose the ones which would be most significant for her. Using your notes, re-write the story from Lorraine's point of view.

- Imagine you meet up with someone in ten years' time. You haven't seen each other since you left school and you find that your two lives have taken very different paths. Write the dialogue which follows. Then tape it for others in your group.

Events in Lorraine's life	*The narrator's opinion of Lorraine*	*Lorraine's possible thoughts*

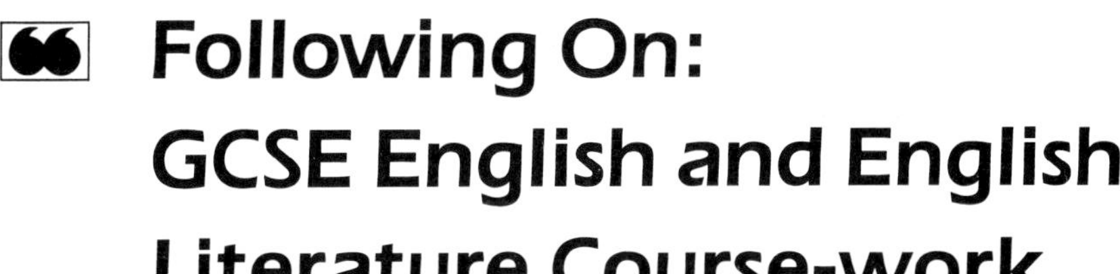

Following On: GCSE English and English Literature Course-work

EXTENDED ASSIGNMENTS

- 'The novel is essentially a nineteenth century form, those wonderful slabs or doorsteps of narrative, of tuppence-coloured characters in motion. Today television does, for better or for worse, what the novel did. Fiction has had to find a new purpose.' In small groups, discuss these comments by writer Giles Gordon. Do you agree with him? Does television work better than a novel or a short story? From your reading in this book, what are the *special* and *common* features and successes of poetry, plays, novels and short stories?

  Compile a chart as follows:

	Special Features	*Common Features*
Play		
Poem		
Novel		
Short story		

  Then write up your findings in an essay.

- Now think about Fionnuala McHugh's style of journalism. What are the special features of writing for a magazine or a newspaper which separate her from the poet or short story writer? Look again at her observations on page 29: 'The other writers are bound by form, the journalist by content'. Talk about this statement in your groups. Write up your conclusions in the form of a comparative study of journalism and storytelling, concentrating on their stylistic differences and similarities.

- Prepare and mount a dramatised reading—complete with sound effects and music—of any of the short stories in this volume. Try to bring out the patterns and contrasts in the narratives, as well as capture the different characters and their attitudes and feelings. Try to bear in mind what Lingard, Geras and Dhondy wrote in their essays about the underlying ideas which they had in mind when writing.

- 'Short stories have much more in common with poetry than with novels. Partly that's because of their compactness, and the way in which they're so tightly controlled. And partly it's because they very often focus on a single place or moment in time'. Use these words from writer Linda Cookson as the starting point for a debate. Try to put yourself in the place of Wendy Cope, Joan Lingard or Adèle Geras. What would each of them have to say on this comparison between the different genres? Rehearse some of your ideas in groups, then write them up in interview format.

- 'A first reading makes you want to know what will happen; a second makes you understand why it happens; a third makes you think'. How true is this in your reading and re-reading of the fiction in this volume? Write up your views as an argument for or against this statement.

- As well as telling a story, writers often want to make us think deeply about an idea, theme or issue. Make a list of the various themes or subjects raised by the six writers. Are there any common elements? Think carefully about what each writer reveals in their essay on the subject of writing for entertainment or education or propaganda. Which of the writers do you feel is more concerned with 'message' than 'entertainment'? This is a complex subject, so talk through your ideas in groups before writing up your findings for your English file.

- Why does someone behave in the way he or she does? What causes someone to take one line of action rather than another? What motivates the characters in this volume? Working in groups, choose one of the stories or the play. Then take it in turns to play the part of one of the characters. Each character is placed in the witness-box and questioned by the others as to why they behaved in the way they did in the course of the action. You might start with Gran in 'White Peak Farm' or Pam in 'The Interview'.

- In writing a novel, short story or play, the author makes certain decisions about what to include and what to leave out. Imagine you can add a couple of extra scenes or episodes to any of the stories or the play in this volume. Follow the style of the original as carefully as you can, and write an extra episode or two.

- Select an incident from one of the stories or the play and write a report of it that might have appeared in the local newspaper. Use interviews as well as reportage, and choose a headline. An extension exercise would be to write *two* reports in different styles, imagining perhaps that one newspaper favours factual reporting while the other tends to sensationalise.

- Choose one of the stories or the play, and write a series of entries in one of the character's diaries which show what he or she thought and felt at different points in the action. Berlie Doherty's play presents many obvious moments.

- If you look at the cover of this book you will see that it has some written information about what the book contains. This 'blurb' can either persuade people to buy a book, or sometimes put them off altogether. Imagine you were writing the cover 'blurb' for a collection of stories, poems, or articles by any one of the writers in this volume. Using the biographical information provided, together with their essays and the samples of their writing that you have read, draft out some cover copy for each writer. Aim for about 400 words as a first draft, and then try to reduce it to 200 words.

- Imagine you are a film director planning to film one of the stories or the play. Before you hold auditions you need to write down a few words about each of the characters to help you choose the right actor for each part. What sort of 'images' do you have of any of the characters you have read about in this book? Draft out brief notes, working with another student.

WRITING ABOUT NOVELS AND SHORT STORIES

When you are writing about short stories and novels as part of your English course, it is useful to be familiar with certain basic 'technical' words. The writers in this volume refer to them in their essays.

1 *Plot*

The plot refers to the *action* in a story. All of us read through a story because we want to know what happens next and how it will end, rather like the way we wait for a punch-line in a joke. When you are reviewing the plot of a short story or novel, think about the following questions:

- How does the story open?
- What time sequence does the action follow? Do scenes follow on from one another or are there flashbacks?
- Do certain moods keep recurring, for example quiet then conflict?
- Are there moments of climax or crisis?
- What are the sub-plots?
- In a novel, do different chapters have a particular line of action or inaction?
- How does the story end? With a twist-in-the-tail?

2 *Setting*

This word refers to the *place* or *period of time* in which the story is set. It is something which the writer can hint at briefly, or can describe in great detail, depending on how important s/he feels setting to be within the total framework of the story. The following questions should be asked:

- When is the story set—the present, past or future?
- Where is it set?
- Is there a special mood or atmosphere to the story?
- How does the location of the story affect the characters and their actions?
- How important is the setting to the author's underlying themes?
- Does the story involve a journey or several changes of scene? If so, produce a diagram to help you understand the movements of the narrative.

3 *Characters*

These are the *inhabitants* of the story. They come in an enormous variety of shapes and sizes: spirits from the past, survivors of disasters, adolescents or aged parents, for example. Sometimes characters are described in great detail; at other times they are only sketched very briefly. Writers often want us to take sides for or against their characters, so they load the dice accordingly. Questions to be asked:

- Who are the main and the minor characters?
- What are they like?
  —physical features, personality, clothes, how they talk, how they feel and behave.
- What are the characters' values and attitudes?
- Are there moments in the story when significant changes to the characters take place?
- Do you side with and like the character? Do you change your mind at any time in the course of the story?
- Do the characters face problems and solve them?

- What does the character do? What does the character say? What is said about her or him by other characters?

4 *Narrator*

Of course, it is the author who actually writes the words, but all stories are told from a particular *point of view*. The writer can do one of the following:

(a) Pretend to be one of the characters in the story and tell everything through that character's eyes. This means that the story will be told using 'I'. This is called 'first-person narration'.

(b) Stand outside the action and look down on it, seeing everything that happens to everyone. Characters are referred to as 'he' or 'she' or 'it', or by their names. This is called 'third-person narration'.

(c) Mix the above two, which requires very clever technical skills.

The essential questions to ask yourself in reviewing are:

- Which kind of narrator is at work? Why has the author chosen this way?
- What are the advantages and disadvantages of each style to the novel or story under review?

5 *Themes*

Writers write to tell stories. We read to find out 'what happens next'. But stories often have important *ideas* or *messages* in them, though we should remember Farrukh Dhondy's warning—'Don't insult the craft of fiction by reducing it to any form of propaganda'.

In reviewing we should ask:

- Why did the author write the story?
- Are there any clear autobiographical or biographical influences and clues?
- Are there any special social, moral or political issues being debated by the author through her or his characters?

6 *Style and Language Usage*

This is something which is often quite difficult to define. It generally refers to the *way* in which a writer tells the story and brings together the various ingredients listed above. A ghost story will be told in a different way from a love story or a detective novel, and all writers have their own habits and tricks of style. When you are writing about style think about the following:

- How long are the sentences and paragraphs? A writer may use longer sentences for detailed descriptions of landscape, but short, sharp sentences when wanting to create tension or suspense.
- How does the writer make us laugh or feel sad?
- What sorts of verbs, adverbs, adjectives does the writer use?
- How does the writer use metaphor and simile?
- How does the writer employ dialogue, conversations and dialect?
- Does the writer use symbolism, and deliberately complex language?
- Does the writer pay close attention to detail or just offer a 'glimpse' of what someone is wearing or where a character is living?
- Is the overall tone factual, sad, unemotional, depressing, shocking etc.?

- Write a short review of each of the three stories in this volume, making sure you include commentary on each of the aspects mentioned in sections 1–6 above.

- Choose one of your favourite novels or a novel you are reading at the moment. Write a detailed review for inclusion in your English or English Literature file. Remember to include quotations from the text to help support your commentary.

- Take each of the above aspects in turn—plot, characters, etc.—and re-read the essays by Adèle Geras, Farrukh Dhondy and Joan Lingard. What does each of them have to say about these 'ingredients' of the story? Compile a chart of your own as follows:

	Adèle Geras	*Farrukh Dhondy*	*Joan Lingard*
PLOT			
SETTING			
CHARACTERS			
NARRATOR			

	Adèle Geras	*Farrukh Dhondy*	*Joan Lingard*
THEMES			
STYLE & LANGUAGE USAGE			

- Now write up your research as *A Study of Three Writers.* You will need to make a careful essay plan before you start and write a rough first draft before completing your final version for your English coursework folder.

- If you have completed the chart above you should now be in a position to recognise certain features about the style of these three writers. Below are extracts taken from other writings by Adèle Geras, Joan Lingard and Farrukh Dhondy. Can you identify which extract is written by which writer? When you have done this, talk in your groups about how you came to your conclusions.
(Answers are on page 96)

A 'That's right. I'm working for Kate's dad in his scrapyard. Remember Kate, Brede's friend?'

'Indeed I do. She used to fancy you, didn't she? Does she go with the job?'

'Sarky as ever, aren't you?'

She made a face at him. 'I think the scrap business would suit you rightly . . . roaming the streets and all that.'

'The streets aren't the same as they used to be. Plenty of scrap lying about, not what we're looking for.'

Scrap in the streets: burnt-out cars and buses and armoured vehicles, torn-up paving stones, barbed-wire coiled to form barricades. And along the streets went soldiers on patrol with fingers on the triggers of their guns, men and women eyeing them watchfully, suspiciously, and bands of children playing at fighting and sometimes not just playing.

B 2:00 p.m. THE KITCHEN, PATTI, SUSAN, ROSE, JEAN, AND THE STRAWBERRY SHORTCAKE

On the whorls and lines of the scrubbed pine table, a blue plate holding a skycraper of a cake: four golden shortcake circles, four snowdrifts of cream, strawberries like spots of blood just visible. Around the base of the cake, pink rosebuds and green leaves. At the other end of the table, Patti sits, and her husband's sisters lean over her shoulders and put their faces near hers so that the eye of the camera can see them all, catch them all, laughing. Happy that the cake has turned out so well. Sixty years married to the same person calls for a cake like this, their eyes say. Patti and Joe will perhaps live to deserve this kind of a cake, but it's too late for Susan and Jean, and as for Rose: who can tell?

C On Wednesday afternoons the café served fish, Bangla-style, and Clive always found it crowded with Bengalis. There was not only the usual young crowd who hung around the café day in and day out, but crews of older Bengali workers who only came for the fish. Clive knew he could pick up leads for several stories from the café. He would have to wait for the business to subside and go in late in the afternoon. Hoshiar Miah, the proprietor, whom the boys called 'Langda Miah', 'the lame one', would always drop him the hint of a story. Some of the boys he knew would fill him in on the goings-on around Brick Lane. He'd pick up things other reporters couldn't get. He had become the *East London Herald*'s Asian specialist, and half his work was done in the Iqbal Café.

D Every cloud is supposed to have one, or so I learned at my granny's knee. Isn't that where you're supposed to learn such things? My granny is full of sayings, most of them rubbish, according to my mother, who has her own sayings. Like most mothers. My granny isn't one of those grandmothers who sits and knits in the chimney corner, shrouded in shawls, if such grannies exist at all. She tints her hair auburn and is employed as manageress at a local supermarket. It's not all that 'super', I must add, as it's only got two aisles, one up and one down, but still, a job's a job these days. And money doesn't grow . . .

E That was true. It was one of the reasons I admired what little I knew of Great-aunt Jonquil. It was at my cousin Primrose's wedding that I last saw her. She arrived late, and waddled down the aisle, past the rows of lacy, pastel ladies, and grey and black men; past the tulle and the voile and the silk; past the gloves and top-hats and the knife-edge creases, like a scarlet Spanish treasure galleon let loose in Henley during the Regatta. From her wrists to her elbows she jingled gold bracelets. Her long dress was plum-coloured brocade, with a pattern of dragons, and on her head she wore something that made the other hats present look like left-over meringues.

F Terry Soakum was a boarder. He was a white boy and came to our class for the first time, ushered by an Anglo-Indian matron, in tears. His arrival caused a quickly quelled stir in the class. There was one other white boy at the school and there had been a third. This third was a Danish boy who spoke no English. He was the son, it was said, of a great Danish engineer who had come to Poona to set up the first penicillin factory in the suburb called Pimpri. This boy constantly smiled, was left alone by most others and came to school in a large chauffeur-driven car. He stayed a year, was of little account and disappeared when his father's expertise was no longer needed in the penicillin plant.

WRITING ABOUT PLAYS

Much of what you have read in the previous section about short stories and novels applies with equal relevance to plays. Indeed, on the *page* plays are very like stories. But there are key differences:

1. The writer places the characters' names in the margin to indicate who is speaking at any one time. Speech marks are not used in a playscript, whereas they are the symbol which the storyteller must use to tell the reader who is speaking.
2. Whereas the novelist blends together the words spoken and how a character might move in saying them, the playwright separates these into 'lines' and 'stage directions'.

And, of course, plays are there to be *performed*. Thus, how an actor interprets the words on the page and how the whole production appears on the stage takes the audience well beyond consideration of plot, character, setting and language style. All of these remain important but further questions need to be asked in reviewing a play at the theatre or on the screen:

- How does the play open? Do the first lines and moments grab the audience's attention?
- How witty or serious is the dialogue? Does it develop the plot and the ideas of the play?
- Are the speeches long and serious or short and witty?
- Is 'movement' on stage appropriate to the words?
- Do the scenes flow naturally into one another?
- Does the acting make the characters credible?
- Do the lighting, music and other effects enhance the production?

■ Bearing in mind the above questions, write your own review of 'White Peak Farm: Gran', highlighting those parts of the script which you feel are more successful than others (a) on the page, and (b) on the screen. You will need to do some visualising of the TV directions for the second part of the assignment.

Tips for writing a play

- After you have completed a first draft, read the script aloud with another student.
- What parts can be improved? Should any characters be added or removed? Can scene-endings be made more interesting?
- Write out a second draft.
- Remember you are writing for *performance*, not silent reading!
- Even once it has been performed you might like to go on rewriting parts to improve the text. Professional writers do sometimes rework their scripts after they have opened in the theatre!

WRITING PLAYS

Here are some guidelines for your own playwriting.

1. Give yourself a wide margin of about one quarter of the width of the paper. This will be for the speakers' names and any rough production notes.
2. Everything which is not spoken should be underlined.
3. Write characters' names in capital letters in the margin.
4. Avoid using too many characters.
5. Avoid using a narrator, but if you must, make what s/he has to say clear and brief.
6. Avoid too many changes of scene.
7. Keep the stage directions brief and precise.

If you are writing a script for radio or television, add:

8. FX indicates sound effects. A radio play is only *sound* so don't write, 'The rising sun lit the field'.
9. All kinds of 'tricks' can be achieved with cameras fading up and down, freeze-framing, etc. so you may want to indicate these.
10. Music can also be indicated on the script.

- Berlie Doherty tells us that 'Gran' is the first of a three-part television series. Read the novel *White Peak Farm* and try turning other parts of it into a television script. If you cannot get hold of the novel, imagine how the first episode develops into the later ones. Write the scripts.

- Turn again to the writings of Geras, Lingard and Dhondy. Choose one of these which you think will make a good playscript, either for radio, television or the stage. Bearing in mind the various tips and notes above, write one of the stories as a play. Avoid using a narrator and remember Berlie Doherty's words: 'If the camera can say it, the characters don't need to'.

WRITING ABOUT JOURNALISM

Hundreds of thousands of words are written and printed each day in our newspapers, and on radio and television journalists file reports from around the world to keep us informed. Just as there are many different kinds of newspapers there are different kinds of journalists, including political correspondents, cookery writers, sports reporters, leader writers and features editors.

As Fionnuala McHugh tells us, 'profiles are a section apart even within the genre of feature writing'. As a freelance writer she turns her hand to many different subjects and for different newspapers, and thus for different audiences. There are clearly certain aspects of writing as a journalist which are different from those we have looked at in previous sections in relation to playwrights and novelists. What they have in common, of course, is that they all want to tell a story.

'Veracity of course is the boundary within which the journalist—unlike the playwright, the novelist, the poet—has to work. The other writers are bound by form, the journalist by content'. This makes for an interesting starting point when we come to ask questions about a piece of journalism.

- Is the journalist revealing the 'truth'?
- Is a 'slant' being put on the facts?
- Is the heading eye-catching?
- Does the article develop ideas logically and thoughtfully?
- Are the paragraphs well put together?
- Does the style of writing suit the subject matter?

- Go back over Fionnuala McHugh's essay. Make a list of what she considers to be the most important qualities of a good journalist.

- Compare what she says about *style* of writing with what other writers in this volume say. What conclusions do you come to about the special features of journalism which separate it out as a genre from writing fiction?

- What is your picture of a journalist? 'A man (still) with a foot in the door and a shifty expression in the eye' (page 26)? Write up your views on the profession of journalism, having shared your thoughts in groups.

- Look at the techniques employed by Fionnuala McHugh in her 'Profile of Kenneth Branagh'. Write your own Profile, either of someone you know well (and could interview) or of someone you would like to meet. With the latter, you will have to make up the interview, and don't forget to include what the interviewee's friends might have said on the phone to you!

WRITING ABOUT POETRY

In *A Defence of Poetry* written in 1821, the Romantic poet Shelley wrote that 'poets are the unacknowledged legislators of the world', and certainly many poets before and since have seen their work as a powerful influence over the affairs of humankind.

There are innumerable definitions of poetry. Some of the more famous ones include:

> 'It is much easier to say what it is not. We all *know* what light is; but it is not easy to *tell* what it is.' (Dr. Samuel Johnson's reply to the question 'What is poetry?')
>
> 'The elevated expression of elevated thought or feeling in metrical form.'
> (Definition from Oxford English Dictionary)
>
> 'Prose = words in their best order;—poetry = the best words in the best order.'
> (Samuel Taylor Coleridge)
>
> 'Poetry is not the thing said, but a way of saying it.'
> (A. E. Housman)
>
> 'Genuine poetry is conceived and composed in the soul.'
> (Matthew Arnold)
>
> 'Poetry lifts the veil from the hidden beauty of the world, and makes familiar objects be as if they were not familiar.' (Percy Bysshe Shelley)
>
> 'If poetry comes not as naturally as the leaves to a tree, it had better not come at all.'
> (John Keats)
>
> 'Poetry is generally esteemed the highest form of literature.'
> (A. E. Houseman)

A writer, as we have seen in this book, writes for a whole variety of reasons—to convey information, to persuade, dissuade, cajole, recreate an experience or record an image that exists in the mind. Unless we are writing with the avowed intention of burning the end product, every time we put pen to paper we are trying to put across some sort of idea, either to ourselves, or more likely so that the reader may learn something from what we have written.

When we read a poem for the first time we tend to make a snap decision about how good we think it is. We assess its subject matter, style and mood, but inevitably on a surface level. It is only with subsequent readings that we may begin to appreciate the full significance of what is being said, and *how* it is being said.

In approaching and writing about a poem there are three overlapping stages.

First, we ask ourselves what the poem is all about; we decide upon its *content.*

Second, we ask ourselves how the poet has achieved her or his particular purpose; thus we examine *style,* which includes handling of diction, metre, rhyme and a whole host of poetic devices.

Third, we must come to some kind of judgement; *is the poem successful,* in its own right or in comparison with the work of contemporaries or writers on the same subject?

This approach suggests we need to have experience of various poets before we can appreciate fully the work of one poet, say, Wendy Cope.

The following technical terms are worth knowing. If you don't know what each one means, try learning them. They will help you to understand and appreciate poetry.

alliteration: the repetition of consonants in words and phrases to give special emphasis.

allusion: a reference to a character, person or event, often indirectly by way of a parallel.

assonance: the repetition of vowel sounds to produce particular effects.

bathos: a sense of anti-climax as one moves from one part of the poem to another.

compound words: double-barrelled words formed by combining two existing words, used to pile up effects or images.

diction: the poet's choice of language, which may be simple, modern, old-fashioned, technical, elaborate.

images: mind's eye impressions which poets use to get their readers' imaginations working.

inversion: reversing the natural word order for the sake of emphasis.

metaphor: a compressed simile. It suggests similarities between two things which are not normally thought to resemble one another.

onomatopoeia: the use of words whose sound echoes the sense they are conveying.

personification: to think of or refer to something which is not human, in human terms. The word is given a capital letter for the purpose.

simile: an explicit likening of one thing to another; the two objects may be very different in their general nature, but similar in one particular way.

symbol: an object which as well as being significant in itself, also represents an idea or abstraction on a higher level.

One last word on technical terms; rhyming patterns are central to many poems (as in Wendy Cope's 'A Policeman's Lot') and each poem needs to be examined closely to establish what kind of rhyme is at work. But remember, poems do *not* have to rhyme, though every one will have *rhythm*, in the way that a song does.

- Reread Wendy Cope's poem. Which of the technical poetic devices listed above can you identify? Discuss these in your groups.

- Thinking about the definitions of poetry given above, write a review of Wendy Cope's poem.

- Again bearing in mind what distinguishes a poem from prose, rewrite 'A Policeman's Lot' as a short story or piece of prose. What differences of style emerge?

- Printed below are two extracts from poems by Wendy Cope. What similarities of style do you notice between them and 'A Policeman's Lot'?

A Here is Peter. Here is Jane. They like fun.
Jane has a big doll. Peter has a ball.
Look, Jane, look! Look at the dog! See him run!

Here is Mummy. She has baked a bun.
Here is the milkman. He has come to call.
Here is Peter. Here is Jane. They like fun.

Go Peter! Go Jane! Come, milkman, come!
The milkman likes Mummy. She likes them all.
Look, Jane, look! Look at the dog! See him run!

B There are so many kinds of awful men—
One can't avoid them all. She often said
She'd never make the same mistake again:
She always made a new mistake instead.

The chinless type who made her feel ill-bred;
The practised charmer, less than charming when
He talked about the wife and kids and fled—
There are so many kinds of awful men.

- Why do you think people write poetry in preference to what you might imagine is an easier form of writing, namely plays or stories? Why does poetry have a 'difficult' image among many students at school? Make a list of poems you have read and enjoyed. What factors have helped or hindered your appreciation of poetry? Discuss these ideas in your groups. Write up your views for your English folder.

YOU AS THE WRITER

You are going to write about *yourself* as a writer in this final section. The whole of this project—charts, notes, transcripts of interviews, essays—can be submitted for your GCSE English file.

Remember what you have learned about various approaches to the craft of writing from the authors featured in this volume!

A *Writing Habits*

Complete a chart.

What I like about my writing	*What I don't like about my writing*	*My writing habits*

In completing the chart, include comments on:

- — when and where you write
- — handwriting
- — using a word processor
- — type of stationery used
- — the way pieces turn out
- — writing for school, friends, yourself
- — criticism from self and others
- — drafting and re-drafting
- — background noise
- — writing on your own, with others, in class
- — reading your own work, reading others' work
- — reading your work out loud
- — planning writing projects
- — writing in different styles
- — writing for different audiences

Tips for writing a personal essay

- Make it personal, perhaps closer to your speaking voice than you would usually do in writing. You could use a tape-recorder for a first draft!
- Be honest about likes and dislikes. Don't write to impress an audience with your studious approach, just make it 'real'.
- Organise it carefully. Work out a plan for your essay in advance. You might start, as Wendy Cope and Adèle Geras do, by talking about your writing history, then move on to influences, likes, dislikes and habits. But it need not be in that order—the choice is yours!
- You may want to keep the whole thing to yourself, but getting other people's opinions and observations on your drafts can be useful.

Complete a time line.

Think about when your writing began. For Joan Lingard it was when she was eleven, for Wendy Cope it was when she was six. When did you consciously start writing? What changes have occurred since? Your time line should begin at the start of your writing 'career' and end at the present day. For example:

7 years → Writing letters to relatives → 11 years → Writing a diary →
Entering a writing competition → 16 years → GCSE folders →

Writing at school.

Look at your writing habits in school-related activities. How does it differ in various subjects? Think carefully about one term or one year in your 'writing history' where great changes took place. It might be moving from the third year to the fourth, with all the demands of GCSE folder-work. Comment on:

- — your different levels of effort
- — your sense of purpose
- — deadlines
- — volume of writing required
- — different audiences you have written for: parent, friends, examiner

Using all of the above background information, write a personal essay which explains your writing habits.

B *The Interview*

When you have completed your essay, ask a relative or friend from a different generation to read it. Now interview them about their own writing habits and opinions. Remember Fionnuala McHugh's technique of giving your own opinion to prompt a reaction in them. Record their reactions and then write this up as an article, which could become a feature in a magazine of your choice. Remember to angle the write-up to what you think the reader will want to hear. Remember Fionnuala McHugh's pointers:

- describe your subject physically
- give explanations of the setting of the interview
- give background information on the character
- give their and your opinions

so that you end up with a sense of the person as well as their words in interview.

C *The Letter*

Decide on a writer who is a favourite of yours and who is still living and working. This can be a poet, novelist, journalist, stand-up comic or playwright. Write a letter explaining your writing project and highlighting the points you have learnt from it. Then ask them about their own writing habits. You could ask specific questions. For example; 'Is the main character in your latest work based on someone you know?', or 'Do you use real settings in your latest book?'

You should also pose general questions about approach and style. Then send the letter off, keeping a copy for your file. You'll be surprised how many people will write back, and if they do you could go on to write a comparative study of their writing habits and yours.

D *Writing Log*

Decide on a piece of writing to complete for your English or English Literature file. It could be a piece of creative writing, a description or an essay in which you argue a point, a poem or a piece of analysis. Work on the assignment and as you do so, keep a log of the way in which you write it. This should include factual information and feelings which may at times be as raw as 'I hate this work' or 'I'm bored and frustrated', and should at the end include some thoughts and reflections on the log.

The log can be submitted alongside the final essay to explain the process you've used.

Tips on making the most of the writing process

- Spend a fair amount of time deciding on the project you wish to complete. Choose something which will maintain your interest through drafting and redrafting.
- Think of something original to do. Don't simply repeat a topic you have done before, unless you have clear aims for developing the idea.
- Make sure you are clear on the exact method employed by the writer you intend to model yourself on. Write it down step by step in your own words.
- Be aware of the *process* of the writing, analysing as you go along, deciding what works for you and what doesn't.
- Keep your eye on the *product* or end result of your writing, and be prepared to change the work in the light of this as you progress.

E *The Writing Process*

Writing to please yourself is an important part of writing successfully. Choose a piece of writing which you would like to complete yourself. It could be on any subject, in any style and using any format. It might be an account of your favourite hobby. Try to make as many decisions as you can about the piece *before* you begin.

If this is to be a GCSE file piece, then briefly explain in a written summary to your teacher what you propose to write, how long you estimate the assignment will take and the methods you intend to use. This will also be useful to you as a statement of aims, so that you know the goals you will be trying to reach.

You could follow the writing process used by any one of the writers in this book.

When the assignment is completed write an evaluation of how well this process worked for you. Think about which methods you would use again and which you would discard, giving reasons for your choices. Were there any which you did not perform completely which you think might have worked had you done so, for example, a second draft before the final version?

F *Self-Assessment*

The writers in this book have different opinions about the writing process, but they all show that style is personal and that a *sense of voice* is essential.

Looking back over the tasks in this section, what have they done to help you to establish *your* personal style? Has being aware of what you've done helped you to write more effectively, because you know what works for you? Or has it had the effect, simply, of fragmenting everything so that you can no longer do it?

Ask other people in your group about their experience. Has being aware of the writing process helped or hindered them?

The editors of *Writing And Response* would be interested in receiving any comments about the book. Please send them to:

Roy Blatchford/Jackie Head
c/o The Education Division
Unwin Hyman Ltd.
15–17 Broadwick Street
London W1V 1FP

(Answers from pages 88 and 89. Joan Lingard—A, D. Adèle Geras—B, E. Farrukh Dhondy—C, F.)